# STONED COLD SOLDIER

CHARLES DENNIS

VINGSBO PRESS

LOS ANGELES

I've set myself against being concerned with any more worldly success than I need to function with. . . . Up to a point, I have to be successful in order to operate. But I think it's corrupting to care about success; and nothing could be more vulgar than to worry about posterity.

—Orson Welles

For Colin Fox, the last member of the Stratford platoon

# Table of Contents

# *FOREWORD*

*Stoned Cold Soldier* was my first novel. It also brought Laurence Harvey and Orson Welles into my life. I was 22 and living in London when I first started writing the book. It was the late 1960s and drugs were a way of life. Marijuana was unknown in England and the most common turn-on was hashish, which made its way east overland on the old trade routes from India. In addition to hash, there were African plants – twigs and branches with hallucinatory powers. A secretary at the William Morris Agency, who worked for WMA's Brooklyn-born rock and roll agent, liked to get stoned with me and had access to an incredible trove of mind-altering delights courtesy of her boss.

One Saturday afternoon in April she arrived at my top floor flat in Sussex Gardens bearing a joint stuffed with something she called Congo bush. We had a few hits before she departed for a previous engagement. I was alone by the time the Congo bush kicked in. My flat was on the fifth floor, and I was soon addressing the leaves pushing up against the window. Addressing? More like proselytizing. Railing against the Viet Nam war. I'd never been so stoned in my life. The philgrims flew by on broomsticks. That was when *Stoned Cold Soldier* came into being.

I tried taking notes, but Congo bush was a cruel taskmaster. Very little made sense when I attempted to decipher my scribblings the next day. This wouldn't deter me from writing a serious protest about the conflict in Vietnam. It was intended to be in the tradition of *Johnny Got His Gun* or *All Quiet on the Western Front*. However, when army chaplain Isadore Feldman was blown up playing the seventh hole of the Inter-Faith Golf Tournament - on the very first page – the comic tone of the novel was set.

Never having served in the armed forces, where was I to find inspiration for the military types? I had worked at Canada's Stratford Festival and forged strong bonds with several actors there. Determined to eventually dramatize the story, I cast the roles with some of my favorite thespians: William Hutt was the inspiration for Fitzroy Claypoole; Colin Fox's comic genius manifested itself in Burnett Remington; and Ken Welsh, the company's *jeune premier* would be the accused, Tommy

Bennett. (Twelve years later, the four of us would appear in the movie *Covergirl*, whose screenplay I had written.) Jimmy Blendick's inner grizzly bear brought Cleet Fowler to life. For The Murder Man, Frank Graham, I shamelessly stole the persona of Stratford alumnus, John Vernon.

The story possessed and obsessed me. I wrote day and night. By June it was completed. My agents submitted the manuscript to every publisher in London without any success.

At the same time, my friend and mentor, Bill Hutt, had taken a sabbatical from the Stratford Festival where he'd been a leading player since the company's inception in 1953. In the summer of 1969, he was a guest star at the Chichester Festival. I took the train south from London to visit Bill and went to a cocktail party where I met another of the festival's guest stars, Laurence Harvey.

Born Larushka Mischa Skikne in Joniskis, Lithuania on October 1, 1928, Harvey was the youngest of three boys. The Skikne family emigrated to South Africa six years later. Lying about his age, Larushka joined the South African army at 15 where he was assigned to the entertainment unit, serving in Egypt and Italy. At war's end, he emigrated to England where he abandoned his Jewish identity and reinvented himself as the quintessential WASP, Laurence Harvey. He led the life of a Regency rake living beyond his means. Put under contract by James and John Woolf, he starred as Romeo in their 1954 Romulus production of *Romeo and Juliet*. This led him to Hollywood where he played the juvenile lead opposite Rex Harrison, George Sanders and Virginia Mayo in *King Richard and the Crusaders*. The movie was a flop and Harvey returned to England and the British film industry.

1959's *Room at the Top* was a role tailor-made for the relentlessly ambitious actor. As social-climber Joe Lampton, he forsook his married lover (Simone Signoret) for a rich man's daughter. The movie was an international hit and Harvey was nominated for a Best Actor Oscar. The man known as 'Laurence of Lithuania' returned to Hollywood and big budget movies including *Butterfield 8, The Alamo, Summer and Smoke* and *The Wonderful World of the Brothers Grimm*.

But it was John Frankenheimer's 1962 suspense classic, *The Manchurian Candidate,* that would be his enduring cinematic legacy. His aloof, cold-as-ice performance as brain-washed assassin Raymond Shaw was quintessential Laurence Harvey. The film would mark the zenith of his career as a movie star. Except for *Darling* and *Life at the Top* (continuing the saga of Joe Lampton), he spent the rest of the decade making movies for money.

When I was introduced to Harvey at the cocktail party, he was dressed in a powder blue safari suit with a cigarette holder dangling from his lips. I audaciously asked him if he'd like to read the best political thriller since *Manchurian Candidate*.

"Can I read it tonight?" responded Harvey.

Larry (as I came to know him) loved the book and suggested Orson Welles direct it. I was speechless. This was too good to be true. Welles had directed Larry and Jeanne Moreau over a three-year period in a movie called *The Deep* that was never completed. Larry shared the manuscript of *Stoned Cold Soldier* with his pal, author Wolf Mankowitz, who was equally effusive in his praise. When would the cameras start rolling?

That evening was spent in Larry's hotel suite where he held court regaling us all with hilarious anecdotes. A superb raconteur, his warm and friendly personality was the antithesis of his screen image. When room service of the Chichester hotel failed to respond to his requests, he branded the management anti-Semitic. Having rediscovered his Jewish roots and a supporter of Israel after the Six Day War, Egypt promptly banned his movies. In a brilliant impersonation of that other Laurence – Olivier – he let loose an ear-piecing howl: "Ohhhh! That I had remained a Christian!"

Larry recounted his first adventure in Hollywood when he was unable to lift George Sanders from the floor during the making of King Richard and the Crusaders. The hilarious explanation of Sanders immobility became the centerpiece of my play, *High Class Heel*, years later.

Returning to London, my agent informed me he'd finally found a publisher for *Stoned Cold Soldier*. Two ex-Guards Officers – whom I dubbed the Two Michaels - had formed a publishing company called Sesquipedalian Press. They were interested in my first book as their first book. Interested but not committed.

Larry Harvey to the rescue! To seal the deal, he took me and Michael One, the slippery partner, to lunch. (Michael Two was the money source and spent most of his time drunk.) Over our meal, Slippery Michael confided how he'd only met one other film star.

"Who was that?" purred Larry, fitting a cigarette into his ubiquitous holder.

"George Lazenby."

I prayed Larry wouldn't get up and walk away. Instead, he took a deep drag on his cigarette and said: "Really!"

The Two Michaels signed the contract, and I was about to become a published author.

Several months passed with no publication date in sight. Slippery Michael told me not to worry too many times for comfort. I went to confront him in his girlfriend's spacious Knightsbridge flat. A third and final notice demanding payment from the printers in Frome, Somerset was in plain view on the dining table.

"What are you going to do about this?" I asked, fearing yet again that my book would never see the light of day.

"I sent him a case of rather inferior port to placate him," drawled Slippery Michael. It was a line one of Evelyn Waugh's characters might have said. Coincidentally, Waugh was Slippery Michael's godfather.

The five hundred copies of my book were subsequently seized by the Sheriff of Somerset and languished in a jail cell. Slippery Michael disappeared.

Two years later the books were rescued by Bachman & Turner publishers, who purchased them from the printers. Larry Harvey wrote a glowing blurb that preceded the book's remarkable reception by the British press. Attached to his blurb was a note:

"I'm really delighted and thrilled for you and feel almost personally rewarded for having had so much faith in your novel from its inception. Handled right, it could be a big success, and I hope that those idiotic critics will concur with my own feelings. I do hope that I have remained within the bounds of sanity in discussing your book, but I mean it."

Larry's note was dated May 31, 1973. Five months later, he was dead of cancer at the untimely age of 45. I've never forgotten his loyalty and affection in writing to me while amid his cancer treatment.

The following year, I was living in Los Angeles. Orson Welles was staying at the Westwood Marquis, where I dropped off a copy of the book with a note telling him of Larry's interest in his directing the movie version.

Two weeks elapsed before I received a phone call from a rumbling voice identifying himself as Orson Welles. When I realized it was really Orson Welles and not someone impersonating him, he was bubbling over with praise about the book. "It's wonderful. I love it. What else have you written?" My second novel, *The Next to Last Train Ride*, had just been published and Welles insisted I send him a copy immediately. I jumped in my car and drove to Westwood.

When several weeks elapsed and I'd received no call from Welles, I called his hotel and was put through to his room.

"What do you want?" thundered Welles as if I were some annoying bill collector. "Why are you bothering me?" He slammed down the phone and I never heard from Orson Welles again.

The book was a great success in Britain and the subsequent paperback version went into a second printing. But there was never an American publication. My agent said Viet Nam was too sensitive a subject for U.S. audiences. *Catch-22* and *MASH* were old wars. This one was still raging.

Fifty years later the book is finally available thanks to Ulrika Vingsbo, Vingsbo Press and Amazon Books Publishers. Rereading the novel now has been a journey back in time where I've been allowed to view a precocious and passionate version of myself with so much to say. I'm glad that boy survived the experience and went on to write so many more books.

Charles Dennis
El Rancho Del Navitas
Shadow Hills, California
March 26, 2024

# THE PLATOON

You just don't lose a platoon; not a whole platoon; not lost.

But that appears to have been the fate of the Wichita Platoon, who'd gone on a simple search-and-destroy mission seventy-five miles North-East of Saigon.

Three days later, they still hadn't returned.

Normally, no one would bother making a federal case out of this. Knowing the Wichita Platoon, they probably got lucky in one of the villages. But the Wichita Platoon was also the Wichita Ball Club and the stupid bastards had screwed up the B Company World Series by not getting back in time.

The Saturday game was canceled and most of the noncoms sat around the PX that night waiting for the boys' return to give them shit. It was generally assumed the platoon didn't come back Saturday night to escape going to services Sunday morning.

The Sunday Morning Service was an interdenominational outdoor affair organized by one Francis 'Tightass' Kelly, who was the biggest prick on the base.

Fitzroy Claypoole, the company commander had been cool regarding the subject of services. 'Every man is answerable to his own conscience' became a convenient phrase, which allowed most of the base to enjoy a delightful sleep-in Sunday morning. The chaplains made a few obligatory grumbles for the first two weekends then grew used to the idea, eventually liked it, and ultimately took advantage of it by organizing an Inter-Faith Golf Tournament (which disintegrated out of respect for the memory of thirty-two-year-old Rabbi Isadore Goldman, who was inadvertently blown to pieces on the seventh hole when he stepped on a Viet Cong land-mine).

Rabbi Goldman's premature demise saw the emergence of Corporal Francis Kelly from King of Prussia, Pa., whose prior claim to prickdom had been known only to the Wichita Ball Club.

Kelly was one of the President's forgotten Americans, a member of the silent majority. The brushed-cut, six-foot, red-haired, pimple-ridden, Jesuit, interpreted the demolition of the likeable rabbi on the seventh hole as a divine symbol. A warning from the Lord that a definite blanket of immorality was smothering the base in general, B Company in particular, and unequivocally the Wichita Ball Club. Father Doolan, the Catholic padre, publicly expressed disbelief that the Lord would have any particular reason for striking down a Jew on Sunday and privately informed Kelly he was 'full of shit'. Needless to say, Father Doolan was the best liked god-man on the base.

The Wichita Ball Club was an obvious target for Kelly's wrath. Natural born shit disturbers of an almost devout irreverence, their favorite target was the devout Pennsylvanian.

Those two erudite young sons of Manhattan, Thomas Jefferson Bennett and Kip Mendlsohn, won Kelly's undying hatred by tipping off PFC Harvey Edelman that Tightass was a transvestite. Edelman broke the story in his 'Gloria Gleam Gossip Column' (one of the six columns the St. Louis native wrote under various pseudonyms in the base newspaper—which he also edited). Kelly soon found himself beset by numerous suitors in the B Company shower house.

Kelly loathed Buzz Kaplan for his immoral, lewd, lascivious, filthy, disgusting, suggestive acid rock record collection—the best discs in South-East Asia. He hated Fingers Mackenzie for his general blasphemous nature, his scheming ungodly ways, his worship of Mammon, and the snakes he was always placing in Tightass's bed.

He hated Dalton C. Keller, the financial wizard of the platoon, who had introduced the Wichita Light shows that had given the platoon its name. The night before Keller's departure overseas, he spent an out-of-sight night with a turned-on chick from Wichita, Kansas, who staged her own light show with a blue plastic garbage bag.

The groovy lady from Kansas twisted the bag like a licorice stick, knotted the ends, and tied it on to a hanger. She then suspended the hanger from the ceiling and set fire to the bottom of the bag.

The bag slowly burned, emitting a science-fiction-like laser-beam and an unearthly noise to match. This Wichita Light Show was best appreciated when the spectators were stoned, which was more often than not.

This was how the vengeful Jesuit knew when the Wichita Platoon was turning on. Kelly wouldn't have known what a joint was if it had stood up and said 'Allan Ginsberg' to him. He did know when the laser-beam shot through the night, marijuana was happening.

When the boys discovered Kelly knew their m.o., they simply lit double-length plastic bags in the barracks and went off into the jungle to get high. Kelly would arrive with the MPs only to discover a hanger suspended mysteriously from the rafters and a strange pool of plastic on the floor.

Tightass's spiritual vendetta also extended to Big Ralph Rolingo, a karate-chopping rounder from Baltimore, who would casually deal the Jesuit a paralyzing blow on the back of the neck in the mess hall. Determined to turn the other cheek to Rolingo's assaults, Tightass was unable to move his neck.

Kelly's dislike of Jaime Ramirez, Punjab, and the Asp was much more basic. Like many patriotic Americans, Kelly was a hopeless bigot. His bigotry didn't bother Ramirez, a Mexican immigrant who didn't understand English very well. Punjab and the Asp were another story.

Punjab and the Asp were the affectionate nicknames for Arthur Lee Haynes and Millard Fillmore Dixon, two African Americans from Detroit, who played shortstop and right field respectively on the ball team. Tightass once made the unfortunate mistake in the heat of anger by calling them 'niggers'.

The remark lost him his two front teeth, his sense of smell for six months, and gained him a limp that Dr. Markson said might or might not be permanent.

The Ball Club decided to let bygones be bygones and sent Kelly a fruit basket, gingerly wedging a baby tarantula between the mango and the papaya.

Dr. Markson managed to treat the bite in time but not before Kelly discovered a significant film review in 'Randall Crane's Cinema' (another of Edelman's incarnations). The nouvelle vague Crane suggested that a scene in an obscure Scandinavian film which had taken place on the seventh hole of a golf course had strong religious connotations. Kelly's imagination took wing. The idea for the outdoor chapel was born. On the day he was discharged from the hospital, the Jesuit went to see Colonel Claypoole.

Tommy Bennett assured his friends: 'He'll never con Fitzroy.'

But Tightass did con Claypoole, and the Colonel ran the show. Fitzroy Claypoole was a frustrated ad man. Born with a gift for the right phrase, it was Claypoole who devised: 'Let a child know that you love him—from a distance' when the subject of civilian fraternization had arisen. When incidents of venereal disease had increased, it was Claypoole who cautioned the men: 'You can have all the windows you like in your house—but be sure those windows are locked.' As the Colonel had been responsible for 'Every man is answerable to his own conscience' it was only right and proper he should meet Kelly's needs with: 'See God as He would like to see you.'

Thus, the outdoor chapel.

Kelly insisted on the Wichita Ball Club doing the actual physical construction. Claypoole thought it a capital idea and dispatched the platoon with machetes to hack out a place of worship in the jungle.

Under God's open sky and the meticulous eye of Francis Kelly, the open-air chapel came into being. Not without an attempt by Punjab and the Asp to cut Kelly's head off with a machete. Kip Mendlsohn and Buzz Kaplan tried to get out of work on religious grounds, a convenient double entendre which that old word master Fitzroy Claypoole admired but found rather redundant. Redundancy became a big issue for two days until Kaplan and Mendlsohn discovered Claypoole was from Maryland and rumored to be a friend of the Vice-President. When the Veep's name was mentioned, Buzz and Kip realized they were out of their league and returned to the task of cutting down rubber trees and pulling jungle foliage up by the roots. Bruce 'Fingers' Mackenzie thought he could get a deal on a neon light to put up over the archway. This idea propelled the Pennsylvania Jesuit into a catatonic fit so impressive the boys resolved to buy Kelly a neon light for Christmas.

It is difficult to say what the attitude of the Wichita Ball Club was towards killing. If cornered, the team members wouldn't know if they'd ever killed anyone. Their passions were baseball and getting laid. The latter activity was becoming redundant (even before Fitzroy Claypoole popularized the word) in that they discovered they were all banging the same hookers. Dalton C. Keller came up with the theory that in their all sharing the same doxy they were inadvertently engaging in homosexual acts by proxy. Punjab and the Asp had no idea what homosexual acts were and when Fingers Mackenzie explained it to them, they almost killed Keller. Tommy Bennett stepped in as peacemaker before any real damage could be done.

Keller's suggestion of sodomy, however, had an unusual effect on the Ball Club. Punjab and the Asp were intrigued by the sound of the word 'homosexual' and ran about acquiring similar exotica they could add to their sexual vocabulary. The duo approached David Maxwell, whom they had steered clear of previously because he was English, and they couldn't understand the words he used. Now they cultivated the correspondent as if he were some Eastern guru. Their appetite for 'class dirty words' seemed limitless. Rolingo even swore to Mendlsohn and Kaplan he'd heard the Asp mutter 'lascivious carriage' under his breath when he caught sight of Dr. Markson's new freckle-faced nurse at the infirmary.

The remainder of the Ball Club found their sexual appetites tapering off. The nurse with the wobbly leg whom Fingers Mackenzie finally made after taking her to see *Love Story* seven times proved to be the closest thing to necrophilia he had ever experienced. ('Christ!' he told Buzz Kaplan, 'I think the army rejects them if they even know what an orgasm *is*—never mind experienced one.')

And the hookers! It was becoming a matter of principle. The Ball Club refused to subsidize the Saigon black market, which had a finger into everything remotely connected with any of the wonders that God had wrought during His seven-day binge.

'Safes,' murmured Ralph Rolingo in the middle of a billiard game with Bennett and Keller. 'Who ever heard of a hooker who wanted you to wear safes? In Baltimore, they tell you to bring a friend along for the ride.'

'Humor them,' said Keller.

'The financial wizard has not comprehended the economics of the situation,' Ralph explained to Tommy. 'The handbook informs us that contraceptives are sold at the PX. But the black market knocks over everything before it even gets delivered. You *have* to buy from them. Five bucks for one safe!!'

Economics wasn't the only thing that put them off the Saigon hookers. Aestheticism. They simply didn't dig these women. Ah! Exception: Cashbox.

There wasn't a Soldier in B Company who didn't go to sleep dreaming of Cashbox. Rumor had it Tightass Kelly once called her name out in his sleep. That rumor was probably started by the same lying s.o.b. who said PFC Harvey Edelman had made her. The possibility of the St. Louis scribe even touching the marvelous girl's skin drove them into periods of overpowering melancholy until they tracked down the source of the rumor: Gloria Gleam alias Randall Crane alias Harvey Edelman. Fingers retaliated by stealing the ribbon from Edelman's typewriter.

Why was this young woman the Eldorado of their sexual desires? The answer lay in her name. Shakespeare, you prick, you hit the nail on the head. Lira. Gelt. Shekels. The golden calf. Pirate's treasure. The board of directors. Havana cigars. Rolls Rice (more than one). Say the secret word you get a hundred dollars: The secret word is a hundred dollars.

The one person they even vaguely knew who'd been with her was David Maxwell, who was on a fat expense account from a big American magazine.

The only guys who knew Maxwell were Punjab and the Asp. They weren't interested in Cashbox.

'Why don't we go up to him?' asked Tommy when he spotted Maxwell squirting a gin and tonic down his throat in a servicemen's club.

'And say what?' asked Kaplan. "Excuse me, Mr. Maxwell. You don't know me, but I understand you've made it with Cashbox. What was it like?" Forget it, Tommy.'

Thoughts of Cashbox and sex were abandoned while the boys devoted all their energies to baseball. Good as they'd been before, they were even better now. They might even take the pennant for the B Company league. First, they had to beat their deadly rivals, the Montana Cowboys.

The Montana Cowboys had two great passions: baseball and killing. The two were intertwined in their thick rodeo minds. They lived to go on patrol and 'hog-tie them Victor Charlies'. Whoo-wee! It was rumored that Cleet Fowler, their pitcher, could throw a cannister of napalm three hundred yards. Batters facing a three-and-no count against Cleet Fowler knew what it was like to be in a Vietnamese mud hut.

It was no secret Fitzroy Claypoole had a more than casual interest in the Montana Cowboys. The Colonel dreamed of leaving the army one day and taking the Cowboys back to the States to play exhibition games. David Maxwell had suggested in one of his articles that Claypoole take the Cowboys on a tour of South America where they could play other veterans whose tactics were equal to theirs. It was rumored Maxwell would receive the Pulitzer Prize for that one caustic line. Either that or have his visa revoked.

When asked by PFC Harvey Edelman (writing one of his rare editorials under his *own* name) to comment on the latter possibility Maxwell answered with one word: 'Redundancy.'

It wasn't merely the desire to carry the torch of Abner Doubleday round the bases that spurred the Wichita Platoon on. No. It was Fingers Mackenzie, the Horatio Alger of Saigon, the last exponent of American drive and initiative, who refused to surrender in the face of the all-powerful black market. He never gave up the belief that he would make a killing in Viet Nam if it killed him and pull off one great swindle in the best American tradition. Unfortunately, the only thing he'd done in his fifteen months in the Orient was to corner the typewriter ribbon market. And the only person who ever used a typewriter was PFC Harvey Edelman. It was a hollow victory at best when Fingers charged him an extra seventy-five cents for a blue and red ribbon.

The Ball Team became Fingers' *raison d'être.* Playing the Montana Cowboys would be a coup. Every dollar, yen and franc in South-East Asia would be riding on that game. Odds were fantastic. The California and Alaska gold rushes would be eclipsed by the monies that would pass hands on that game.

'You mean throw the game?' asked Rolingo, whose father had been a bookie in Baltimore.

'We won't have to', answered Fingers with religious fervor. 'We can beat those goddam storm troopers blindfolded. Punjab's the greatest shortstop I've ever seen in my life. And you, you crazy karate bastard, no one can hit a ball as far as you can.'

'What do you want the money for?'

'Ralph, Ralph, Ralph. Don't you see?' Fingers was all but trembling now. 'Let's say we make 5000 bucks on the game. Five thousand, Ralph. That's a lot of bread. We go and see Cashbox. The whole team. And have the best, most expensive, most well-earned gang bang in the history of the republic.'

It was akin to the Sermon on the Mount. Ralph carried Fingers' words back to the Ball Club. Their eyes grew larger in their sockets. Their knees buckled under them. They fell to the ground in one of the most spontaneous mass religious demonstrations in the memory of modern man. Had Father Doolan passed the barracks at that moment, he would have referred to the tableau in his own characteristic way as 'a goddam miracle'. It wasn't just the idea of sex after a long period of abstinence. What the hell! there was always the showers. No, no! It was more than that. It was what the whole war was about. What all wars were about, what democracy meant. Cashbox couldn't stand contraceptives!

One can well understand why the men were massed in the PX Saturday night waiting for the Wichita Platoon to return. With the Wichita Platoon went all their dreams and fantasies—albeit by proxy. The Ball Club were potential heroes to the men. As with all heroes, it is not what they do that stirs us. We project a part of ourselves unto all heroes and it is that projected conceit and pride which makes us hero-worshippers. When the straws would be picked for the order of the assault, it wouldn't simply be Private Tommy Bennett or Private Kip Mendlsohn who would plant the flag. When the source of their manhood entered the cotton-candy cave of that slant-eyed beauty, they would carry the hopes and dreams of every American soldier everywhere.

What's the sense of talking about it? The stupid pricks went and got themselves lost.

On Monday morning a huge Quonset hut appeared in the jungle five hundred yards outside the base. Like Kubrick's monolith in *2001*. Nobody knew how the hell it got there, but it loomed ominously on Monday morning surrounded by a barbed wire fence and an 'Authorized Personnel Only' sign.

Quarantine.

The word spread throughout the base. Stupid bastards had obviously contracted some fucking disease while on patrol and gotten themselves quarantined. Twenty members of the Wichita Platoon—relief pitchers include. What would happen to the ball game? How long would the quarantine last? For the members of B Company, it was the worst thing to happen to them since they'd been inducted.

Even Father Doolan had been forbidden to visit the quarantine area. He simply muttered 'that cocksucker Claypoole'. That was all anyone could get out of him. The men were certain if Rabbi Goldman was still alive, he'd have found a way to get a message from the Ball Club. Someone suggested asking PFC Harvey Edelman of St. Louis, Mo., if he knew anything but discovered someone else had told Edelman about the quarantine.

A general malaise overtook the camp. The men stopped eating which curiously ended the daily queues at the infirmary. The only person Dr. Markson had to talk to was Maxwell, the Englishman, who came in for his daily crabs check-up. Even the Montana Cowboys were affected by the quarantine. Not out of any affection for the Wichita Platoon. At best they thought of the rival team as 'a collection of weirdo, leftist troublemakers—who had coons on their team to boot'. No, it was simply that Cleet Fowler had looked forward to the possibility of blinding one of the Wichita Ball Club or at least crippling one of them for life. It just wasn't meant to be.

Someone suggested praying. Tightass Kelly found his chapel filled to overflowing mornings and evenings. People were coming to pray for the Wichita Ball Club. Tightass realized he had sinned and was ashamed. The Ball Club were agents for good. Not evil. He had been blinded by his own vanity. The Ball Club was responsible this capacity house—flock. Tightass prayed for the recovery of the Wichita Ball Club.

His prayers inspired the pilgrimage to the Quonset hut. At the climax of the evening service, Tightass urged all his brothers and sisters—just what he meant by the last word is still in doubt with an all-male congregation—to follow him into the jungle where they would sing hymns of encouragement to the quarantined soldiers. Upon reaching the barbed wire, they were greeted by twenty M-16 rifles. The celebrants were declared AWOL and ordered back to the base.

Tightass made it clear his orders came only from the Lord. Which resulted in Francis Kelly losing the middle and index fingers of his right hand and being sent Stateside with a Purple Heart.


The only person unconcerned with the fate of the Wichita Ball Club was David Maxwell.

Maxwell's only thoughts were of crabs and Dr. Markson's presence on Okinawa for the past five days. The Englishman had been left to face the crabs alone. Desperate to preserve his sanity, Maxwell sent daily telexes to Markson in Okinawa threatening to report the doctor to the American Medical Association for failing to contain venereal disease in South-East Asia.

Dr. Markson was finally back. Good old Milton Markson. Tufts '52. Dragged out of a fantastic private practice for the two-year military service he'd copped out of during the Korean conflict. His wife, whose political leanings made Martha Mitchell look like Jane Fonda, had sworn never to sleep with him again if he didn't give his country the service he owed them. Milton knew he couldn't live without balling Estelle—even after fifteen years of marriage.

'Why don't you cheat on her?' Maxwell would ask.

'You writers!' Markson would say in his foghorn voice, shaking his head sadly, 'that only happens in books.'

Maxwell knew Dr. Markson was an idiot, but he was also convinced the medico was the only man who could prevent him from catching crabs.

'Migod, it's good to see you again,' said Maxwell, kissing Markson's stethoscope and dropping his trousers. 'Tell me the worst. I can take it.'

'Did you ever play basketball?' asked Markson, prodding Maxwell's inner thighs. 'You've got fantastic muscles here.'

'Please, Milton, don't put it off. How long have I got?'

'You *are* married, aren't you?' asked Markson with a twinkle in his eye.

'Milton, you know I'm not married.'

'Oh, I know that's what you say,' replied Markson. 'But you're always having intercourse.' Maxwell looked at him questioningly. 'You're not allowed to have intercourse unless you're married.'

'Milton, you're an idiot.'

Milton Markson began to cry.

'Milton, I'm sorry. I didn't mean to say that. It's just—well, didn't you have intercourse before you married?'

'Why do you think I wear glasses?' sobbed Markson.

Maxwell felt it best to drop the subject. Besides his attention had been diverted by three Vietnamese nurses kneeling in prayer in Markson's waiting room. Maxwell grimaced.

'Pain? asked Markson.

'No. This bloody Wichita Ball Club cult. It's getting out of hand.'

Markson had no idea what the correspondent was referring to. Maxwell filled him in quickly. The doctor shook his head in disbelief.

'I am the chief medical officer on this base and I assure you there is absolutely no quarantine you speak of.'

Maxwell told him about the Quonset hut; the doctor knew nothing about it. Markson called in his assistant Captain Collins. The younger doctor said there was nothing in their records about a quarantine.

Maxwell pulled up his trousers and lit a cigarette. He had forgotten about his crabs. A smile came over his face.

'I came to Viet Nam looking for a story,' said Maxwell. '*The* story. I think I've found it.'

# *THE CORRESPONDENT*

Crabs.

It wasn't a fixation. It was a deep-rooted fear. Maxwell was terrified it was his destiny to get crabs and die. He'd never believed in destiny until 1955 when he decided to make his living as a writer. He read about all the other writers who had died—for want of a better word—unnaturally. That Percy Bysshe Shelley had drowned was a fact Maxwell never fully recovered from. The simple act of taking a bath remained a liquid form of Russian roulette forever after. Margaret Mitchell's death in an automobile crash put him off driving for two years. Socrates taking hemlock drove him to a microscopic examination of any liquid refreshment or medicine with which he came in contact. There was an innocent almost childlike quality to his 'writer's destiny' theory. As if those long dead legends might still be alive if they hadn't gotten themselves killed.

Maxwell eventually overcame the hang-up in 1956 when an Egyptian mortar shell exploded near him in Suez, killing four men and leaving him unscathed. For several months afterwards, he was convinced of his immortality. Destiny was hurled to the winds. Following his demobilization, Maxwell decided his steps were too large to bestride the map of England. His childhood romance with Helena had turned into a bloody awful marriage, a rather messy abortion, but an extremely convenient affair for her with a frightfully nice chap from the Inland Revenue while Maxwell had been off losing the last vestiges of the Empire in Suez.

In 1957 David Maxwell left Fleet Street, a remarried Helena and England behind him as he passed beneath the Statue of Liberty's kindly, well-shaped underarm.

Little did Maxwell know that those inspiring, sea-sprayed moments as he entered the port of New York would mark the end of his innocence.

Within hours of disembarking, he would find himself sweating it out in the office of the awesome and dreaded Ethel Kane Kirtsin, the self-appointed cultural guardian of America. God help the round socialistic peg that tried to find its way into Mrs. Kirtsin's square hole. There would be no mercy. Only a swift about-face and back on the boat. For this young English journalist, who'd foolishly admitted to being a member of the British Labour Party, what hope could he have of obtaining an alien residency—a green card? Hercules himself would have crapped out at the thirteenth labor: successfully completing one Mrs. Kirtsin's scientifically prepared cultural 'investigation and response' forms.

It would all be over before it began, thought Maxwell thought as he sat outside Mrs. Kirtsin's inner office. There was no hope, no mercy, no chance at all. Damp. He was damp. Beads of perspiration. Streams. Rivers. Torrents. Fingers atremble. Death was imminent.

For a moment, Maxwell feared a recurrence of the malaria he'd suffered briefly in Suez. As a distraction, he focused his gaze comfortably on the fantastic legs of Mrs. Kirtsin's secretary. They went all the way up. Endless. Perched behind the desk was the loveliest honey blonde sitting ridiculously far back from her typewriter as though she feared the keyboard might assault her at any moment. There was no card on the desk to reveal her identity. Maxwell was loathe to chat her up with the only phrase that came into mind: 'What sort of ribbon do you use?' He'd been warned about American women's misconception of an Englishman's virility. Any reference to typewriter ribbons this early in the relationship could be misconstrued as erudite, effeminate, or—God forbid! the harbinger of impotence. Ribbons would have to wait. There would be many, many evenings to come when they could sit by the fire, and he would tell her the sheer joy of walking into Straker & Bedser's to purchase their best black-and-red for half a crown.

His destiny had never seemed so full. His expectations outpipped Pip's. Here was William Penn about to be presented with a Sylvania. Barely three hours in America and a woman loved him. And he loved her, nameless as she was. Raising her hand to touch her hair, Maxwell noticed she had the same kindly, well-shaped underarm as the Statue of Liberty. How had he failed to notice what a sensual woman Miss Liberty was? But why hadn't the sculptor shown her legs? Those same legs that could spread so seductively to take in the tired and hungry, the homeless longing to be free. Little did he know that Miss Liberty was suffering from crabs.

The valley of the red, white, and blue vanished from sight as Ethel Kane Kirtsin emerged from her office. Maxwell knew how Sinbad felt when the Roc burst out of its shell.

Mrs. Kirtsin was a no-nonsense woman possessed of a face which outeagled the republic's best eagle. Realizing this woman would ask him if he was a writer. Maxwell was terrified of the imminent result. He heard D. H. Lawrence emit his last tubercular cough, saw F. Scott Fitzgerald reaching out for that last drink. There are books I still haven't written! Maxwell wailed within himself as he followed the civil-servant Circe into her lair. Please give me a chance to express myself.

'We have scientifically prepared these forms in order that you might have a chance to express yourself.' Mrs. Kirtsin droned in a non-committal fashion, handing Maxwell several typed forms in triplicate. Mrs. Kirtsin then mentioned the names of ten renowned European artists. Maxwell's face glowed at the possibility of being associated with such fine talent. Mrs. Kirtsin burst the bubble when she callously explained that she had rejected all of their applications. Maxwell heard a far-off whimper. It was John Keats hearing his last unheard melody. Virginia Woolf was filling her pockets with pebbles and walking into the water.

Maxwell was to fill out the form and return with it in a week's time. He sat down in a chair in the outer office, caught his breath and gazed over the forms. They looked straightforward enough. Lists of favorite music, books, and films. Also a few multiple-choice favorites. Quite easy. *Too easy.* Mrs. Kirtsin was the Sphinx defying anyone to come up with the correct answers to her riddles.

'Hey! Know anything about typewriters?'

It was Miss Liberty. She had a voice to match her legs. What had she asked? Typewriters? Did I know anything about typewriters? Foolish girl, they were my first mistresses. Is something wrong with your typewriter, my darling? Do you want David to set it a right? Maxwell felt his strength return. She wants me to fix her typewriter. And I shall. I shall. I'll be so gentle and loving as my fingers fondle your keyboard and caress your marginal release. Is it an Olivetti or an Underwood? No matter. Neither one is a stranger to my touch.

Perhaps it was the suggestion of machinery or one of those naughty nerves that man seldom has control over, but Maxwell became aware of a fantastic hardness pushing against the tweed around his crotch. He began to blush. What will she think of me? Behaving this way. Hopefully, she'll recognize it as the hot flush of passion. What if she mistakes the sudden pinkishness for some orchid-like demeanor? A certain lightness of foot? His position would have to be made clear immediately. But could one do it right here in the outer office? Granted American women were basic—but to what extent?

When he hadn't replied, Miss Liberty flashed a smile at him and asked: 'What are you? Deaf?' Maxwell hadn't heard the question. He'd only seen the smile. The sort of smile Raymond Chandler had written you could feel in your hip pocket. I'm coming to you, my darling. My passionate pioneer. True descendant of Annie Oakley, Calamity Jane and Belle Starr. Maxwell knew what the Declaration of Independence meant as he strode across the room. There was nothing of the Leslie Howard or Robert Donat about him now. No. As he took Miss Liberty in his arms, raised her up from her desk, and crushed his mouth against hers he *was* Robert Mitchum.

Miss Liberty raised her knee swiftly into Maxwell's groin and let out a scream. Ethel Kane Kirtsin flew out of her office and immediately summoned the Security Police. They promptly hustled Maxwell into a cab and on to the first London-bound plane. He was forbidden to ever re-enter the United States.


That is probably what would have happened to anyone else but it certainly would do nothing to help this story progress. David Maxwell is far too important to this novel to have him kicked out of America.

No. After Maxwell kissed Miss Liberty and released his considerably strong grip on her shoulders, she reopened her closed eyes and gasped out an impressed: 'I thought all Englishmen were fags!'

Maxwell suggested an opportunity to prove Bobbi—for that was Miss Liberty's name—wrong. Bobbi suggested dinner that night and advised Maxwell to bring his questionnaire.

Bobbi opened the door to her West Side apartment. Maxwell attempted to plant a kiss on her all too kissable lips, but Bobbi ducked and grabbed the questionnaire from his hand. The table was set and a delicious lasagna came out of the kitchenette.

'Come on, David,' said Bobbi. 'We'll have to work and eat at the same time. It's the only night I have to help you.'

The first question was straightforward: THREE FAVORITE FILMS.

'Easy enough,' said Maxwell. '*Odd Man Out, Ivan the Terrible* and *Les Enfants du Paradis*.'

'Wrong. They're all foreign films. You've got to be crazy to even mention Eisenstein on government paper.'

'What do you suggest?'

'Lassie, any John Wayne film, *Gone with the Wind*. I think *Bambi*'s still all right. I'm not sure about some of the other Disney's.'

'Are you joking?' asked Maxwell.

FAVOURITE ORCHESTRA.

'The London Philharmonic.'

'Wrong. You shouldn't know what an orchestra is. If really pressed try Guy Lombardo and his Royal Canadians.'

FAVOURITE SYMPHONY.

'I don't know what a symphony is,' Maxwell said, thinking he'd finally got the hang of it.

'Not quite,' said Bobbi. 'Just name any Souza march.'

'Nothing here about literature,' said Maxwell scanning the list.

'There's one question,' corrected Bobbi, pointing with her fork. 'The answer is Frances Parkinson Keyes.' Maxwell had never heard of the lady. '*Steamboat Gothic*? Anyhow, Mrs. Kirtsin believes that the only art form of any significance—you know, the only true American art form is the movies. Here! Try the multiple choice.'

WHICH OF THESE THREE FILMS IS BEST SUITED FOR CHILDREN: *From Here to Eternity*; *The Boy with Green Hair*: *Mildred Pierce*.

'*The Boy with Green Hair* appears to be the only children's film on the list,' muttered Maxwell, who was now clueless about America's cultural habits.

'Are you crazy?' asked Bobbi. 'Joseph Losey directed *The Boy with Green Hair*. He's been blacklisted. Here. Give me the form. I'll finish it.'

Bobbi filled out the form throughout dinner then she and Maxwell moved to the sofa and listened to Paul Anka sing 'You Are My Destiny'. Bobbi leaned her head against Maxwell's shoulder.

'Thank you for filling out my form,' said Maxwell.

'Shh,' said Bobbi and put her hand on his crotch. It was an old suit and Maxwell was terrified his erection would burst through the tweed. That and Paul Anka going on about destiny was all he needed. Their lips came together and he was delighted to discover her tongue had more moves than a Swiss watch.

Inside her bedroom, Bobbi made no great rush to remove her clothes. The speed and efficiency of the meal and filling out the form was now a thing of the past. She sat Maxwell down on her bed and began to remove his clothes. He couldn't remember whether she had unbuttoned his shirt or bitten off the buttons one at a time. Maxwell was out of his poor immigrant skull. This was going to be the best. Oh! the screams of pleasure. She'd probably lose her lease, but that didn't matter. He'd take care of her. Always. There'd be no trouble with Mrs. Kirtsin. Destiny, destiny, destiny. Oh, sweet Christ! She's taking her clothes off. Look at those breasts. They're magnificent. The nipples are rising by themselves. Migod! She *is* psychic. Look at her swaying. Oh, that bitch! She knows what she's doing.

Standing by the window with the moon reflecting off the Hudson River and her long blonde hair tumbling down to her shoulders, she was not of this world. She walked towards him, humming seductively as she came.

That was when he noticed she had no hair in an area where most ladies of his experience had hair. Upon closer examination, he realized it had been shaved off. Why?

The moment having been shattered, Bobbi sat down on the bed and explained she had been the mistress of a very famous film star for almost two years. (The film star had been one of Maxwell's boyhood heroes.) When the affair finally ended, she came East. Three months prior to her meeting Maxwell.

'What about . . .?' Maxwell gestured vaguely towards the shaved area.

'Oh, he never balled me. Just liked to eat me.'

Maxwell was dumbfounded.

'Hell,' she had an afterthought, 'no one's balled me in almost two years.'

'Would you like to?' asked Maxwell with the innocent trepidation of a man offering a woman a cigarillo.

'Don't know,' said Bobbi. 'I'm so used to (she mentioned the film star's name).' But she liked Maxwell. So, she tried. And she loved it. Oh, how she loved it! What a waste those two years had been. More, more, more. Fantastic. 'Oh, God,' she screamed out in ecstasy. 'I'm going to lose my lease.'

Bobbi went to stay with her older sister, who had just given birth to twins. Maxwell didn't see her again until the next week when he returned to Mrs. Kirtsin's office with the completed forms.

She feigned detachment until Maxwell reached Mrs. Kirtsin's door. She grabbed his hand, squeezed it and whispered: 'I'm letting my hair grow.'

Ethel Kane Kirtsin was astonished by Maxwell's completed forms. She pronounced them the most inspiring and moving investigation and response forms she had ever read. Though Maxwell had been born and raised in England, in his heart he had always, obviously, been an American.

Bobbi and Maxwell celebrated that night and every night for the next three weeks. They camouflaged her deafening screams of pleasure by playing Miles Davis albums full blast. Maxwell hadn't secured a position with a newspaper since arriving in New York. It didn't really bother him since he was living with Bobbi and she was making enough to support them both comfortably. It was a blissful life for David Maxwell. Except for the one question which continued to gnaw at his self-conscious.

It was the sort of question one might casually bring up over coffee or during the aftermath as she lay with her head on his chest, and he stared blissfully up at the ceiling. It was not the inquiry to make while in the midst. But he made the fatal error and asked: 'Why didn't he make love to you?'

'What?' gasped Bobbi.

'Why didn't he make love to you?'

'Because he had crabs.' She continued writhing in delight beneath him.

Maxwell didn't know what crabs were but realized their significance. Whatever they were, they'd successfully prevented the film star from practicing his manly function and art. The same film star who had cheered young Davie Maxwell through the Blitz with his celluloid exploits, be they as a pirate, fighting Japs in Burma, or—best of all—riding tall in the saddle. Crabs had got him. Impotence. Sapped of that very strength which had made him the idol of boys everywhere. (Years later Maxwell would come to think of crabs as a Communist conspiracy—the only conspiracy theory he would take seriously. That was why he became particularly obsessed with the possibility of incurring crabs in Viet Nam. If the U.S. used napalm, he knew that the Viet Cong would use crabs.)

He felt his strength fade away from him. All too soon he saw Danton's head beneath the blade of the guillotine. Pushkin fell dead the victim of his own brother-in-law's bullet. Sheer panic overtook Maxwell. With what strength he still possessed, he hastily dressed and ran like a madman from the apartment out onto Riverside Drive where he fell over Audrey's car.

Fortunately, the car was parked with Audrey parked in it. Six months later Audrey and David were married. Seven years later they were divorced. In between David Maxwell had become God's gift to American journalism.

Audrey's father, the proud son of an old New England family, secured the young Englishman a position on the *Herald-Tribune*. His Sunday magazine articles were eagerly awaited each weekend by millions of readers. His detachment and wit made him the darling of the smart set on both coasts and both sides of the Atlantic. His four non-fiction novels were all best-sellers.

In 1966 he went freelance for a fantastic flat fee plus expenses. His friends told him he was mad. No American magazine would pay that sort of money. But those friends were Americans, so Maxwell had the advantage of detachment in understanding how their minds worked. He became swamped with offers. He rejected the offbeat stories and the 'fun' articles choosing to go after 'challenges' instead. People began to joke that Maxwell could change any average story into a challenge to meet his own needs. He was often referred to as 'the Frank Graham of literature'. Maxwell didn't mind the comparison as he had great admiration for the celebrated criminal lawyer whom his colleagues referred to as The Murder Man.

By the beginning of the Seventies, Maxwell was beginning to worry. Not about money. More than enough of that was socked away in a numbered Swiss bank account. Aside from the crab phobia, he was in the best of health and had magically kept his looks.

Why the worries? The elusive word: destiny. What if the crabs didn't get him and a plane crash did? All those flying hours without a hitch. It was only a matter of time. What would his legacy be? He didn't mean best-sellers. He meant 'a great work'. What writers from the year dot have referred to as *the* story.

Having completed the challenge of two months at NASA headquarters in Houston (where one of the big boys in mission control lamented: 'We don't mind being misquoted but this goddam Englishman knows shorthand. He writes down everything. Belch once he'll put it in italics!') Maxwell concluded that the Viet Nam war was the tragedy of the century. The United States was on the verge of the greatest fall since Milton bounced the Prince of Darkness out of Heaven.

He decided to accept the offer of *Insight*, a new glossy public affairs magazine, that had been pursuing him for weeks to do any series of his choice. They went berserk when he suggested a Viet Nam series. Contracts were drawn up. Worldwide serialization rights were secured. One of the TV networks even suggested a weekly film report by Maxwell.

This was the public-front of Maxwell's presence in Viet Nam. The search for *the* story he discussed only with himself.

After five months in Viet Nam, the search for *the* story seemed a complete failure. His articles had been as successful as ever. Read by the masses. His television personality was one of the surprises of the season— an engaging, witty, and compelling presence.

No, the public front of David Maxwell was as secure and well-respected as ever. It amused him to know he was on his way to becoming an institution. But where the hell was *the* story?

Certainly, it wasn't with those two crazy, black NCOs, who'd been following him around the base gleaning such words as 'auto erogenous' and 'flagellate' out of him. Nor was it with Cashbox. Cashbox, who had almost fallen in love with him, and fled in panic to Honolulu.

Her disappearance caused Maxwell to search even harder for *the* story. He found it easier to get most of his legwork done by tolerating the presence of PFC Harvey Edelman, who was an energetic little prick but had no concept of a scoop. And with Edelman running around the base looking for any sort of news story, Maxwell had very little to do but lie in bed all day and let his libido run rampant. The microfilm of his mind programmed the great lays of his first four decades and he enjoyed this exercise for about twenty minutes. But as a creative artist it simply wasn't enough.

He began frequenting the serviceman's bar, not out of any newly discovered kink in his personality, but to play 'the name game'. The name game had started off harmlessly enough but now obsessed him day and night. He would overhear a soldier mention the name of a girl back home and he would promptly create this girl in his mind, under what circumstances he had met her and what she had been like in bed (or wherever they did it). It was great fun and something, he hoped, that would keep him out of trouble till Cashbox came back.

Elizabeth! big girl, solid arms, great laugh. I met her while riding. Supreme carnal creature. She goes on forever like an electric pony in a supermarket! Ruby! little Ruby. Short kinky hair. I met her in a penny arcade. We did it the first time on a pinball machine. She coincided her orgasms to go with the TILT button. Pamela! Cool, reserved. Met her in the National Portrait Gallery. Pursued her. Said she was incapable of loving. Finally made her in a garage underneath a Porsche. She *was* incapable. Selena! long and lovely. We did it in a canoe. It was so nice and so calm I don't remember what it was like. Melanie! Terribly sincere. She was in the Peace Corps. We did it in a windmill. She cried.

It was a lovely game, harmless and creative. Until it grew out of hand. The same soldiers kept coming into the club talking about the same girls. Maxwell couldn't tolerate repeaters. He began making up his own names and playing the game at home. Rhoda. Vanessa. Constance. Ambrosine. Lulu. Phillipa. Francine. Teresa. By day's end, he was a wreck. He'd so psychologically convinced himself he'd been with these girls, his body responded in a like manner. He was exhausted. Could barely walk. Then it hit him. How did he know these girls were clean? How did he know they didn't have—oh, God! He fell into a deep sleep which lasted almost two days. He didn't dream. His mind saw only cool, clean, whiteness. Towards the second day he heard a voice. An anonymous voice calling out a name: Estelle, Estelle, Estelle.

A new curse. A new affliction. He was obsessed with Estelle Markson, a woman he had never met. Never seen. But a woman whose sexual stranglehold over a man was strong enough to send him to Viet Nam. Maxwell tried to visualize Estelle. Imagine what she looked like. He knew she was 36 or 37. But that wasn't enough. Was she an old 36 or a young 37? What were her legs like? What did she say in the throes of passion? She must be bloody commanding to keep Milton in line all those years. Obviously, an expert in propaganda. His mother would never have given him that bullshit intercourse story. One was clearly dealing with a fantastically sexual fascist. Maxwell could only envision a much younger Ethel Kane Kirtsin. What the hell did Estelle Markson look like? He couldn't ask Milton for a picture of his wife.

'Got any pictures of your wife?' asked Maxwell during his next visit.
'Why?'
'Thought I might do an article on the women at home.'
'I'll bring one tomorrow.
The next day, however, Markson went to Okinawa. Maxwell was left alone without Cashbox, without Estelle, and with crabs creeping closer every day.

Milton Markson's positive denial of any quarantine on the base burnt through the correspondent's neuroses like acid. His mind was totally clear. This was it. The end of the rainbow. *The* story. How the hell was he going to get it?

There was no sense in denying the Quonset hut. It just sat there. Everyone on the base had seen it. That religious catamite Kelly had lost two fingers over it. Everyone knew about it except Milton. Why the hell didn't they want Milton to know? Mainly because they knew Milton wouldn't lie. When did Milton go to Okinawa? Sunday. The Quonset hut didn't appear till Monday. Today's Thursday. Things were starting to fall into place. Who told me the Ball Club was quarantined? Remington. That idiot Captain Burnett C. Remington. Communications officer. Claypoole's goddam mouthpiece. Of course. What the devil was going on in that Quonset hut if they weren't quarantined? No, no, that's getting ahead of ourselves. Something else has to be done first. Right! The existence of the Quonset hut must be recognized. Wait till the press briefing.

Maxwell hadn't attended a press briefing in over three months. In fact, no one went to press briefings anymore except PFC Harvey Edelman and a rotating trio from the international press pool who only went to keep up appearances. Maxwell's sense of the dramatic, however, required more than an audience of four men.

He reached for the telephone: 'Hello, Harvey. Maxwell here. Listen, lad, I'm over at the infirmary. Meet me here in half an hour and we can stroll along to the press briefing together? . . . Cheers.'

Half an hour was more than enough time for the impressionable PFC Harvey Edelman to let everyone on the base know David Maxwell had invited him to 'stroll along' to the press briefing. Maxwell *never* went to press briefings. Something was up.

Burnett C. Remington looked at his watch and realized he was five minutes late for the press briefing. This didn't really bother Remington. No one would be there except Edelman and the three sleeping correspondents. All Remington had to do was report the number of helicopters repaired in the last week and make up some vague number of Viet Cong casualties. He had informed Fitzroy Claypoole if the Colonel wasn't present at the briefings, no one would know the difference.

Captain Remington almost shat himself when he walked into the recreation hall and discovered 250 members of the press corps impatiently awaiting his arrival. For the first time since entering the service, Burnett Remington was on the defensive.

'Good afternoon, gentlemen,' he said with a voice not too sure of itself. 'Sorry to have kept you waiting. Won't keep you long.' Opening his attaché case, the communications captain removed a few sheets of paper. 'Helicopter repairs in the past week—'

'I'd like to ask a question.'

Remington recognized the Englishman's voice but was afraid to look up. He'd carefully avoided all contact with the man since he'd been in Saigon. Now here he was asking a question surrounded by all the other correspondents. Remington unmasked the papers from his face and stared into the center of the hall where Maxwell nonchalantly held his hand in the air.

'Was there something, Mr. Maxwell?'

'A question.'

'Could it wait until I finish my report?' asked an extremely polite Remington.

The communications officer managed to stretch his report to a record two minutes. Maxwell's hand went up again.

'Could you please make a formal statement regarding the quarantine of the Wichita Ball Club?'

Perspiration broke out on Remington's forehead. He swallowed hard. This was impossible. It couldn't be. Maxwell had found out. He knew.

# *THE MEDIA*

There was no doubt the Quonset hut would eventually become a mythological symbol or, at least, a special issue postage stamp. When the public first became aware of it, it seemed to be an ad for a new Antonioni film.

Imagine turning on the television at half past six and seeing ten minutes of nothing. No, that's not being objective. Sounds like a review of *Red Desert*. The television comes on. Cronkite, Brinkley, one of those pillars of security. The first item he hits you with is the Quonset hut.

Cut to the jungle. Green leaves forming a Gauguin frame around the picture tube. Telephoto lens zooming in on the 'Authorized Personnel Only' sign. Lens pulls back to reveal the Quonset hut. Camera holds on it for ten minutes. No Muzak. No whispering Jim McKay commentary explaining how difficult the jump is going to be. Nothing. Just the frozen Quonset hut. Like an eye chart for orangutangs.

Forty million Americans sitting and watching the bloody thing every night. Waiting for God-knows-what to emerge from it.

Secretaries sipping their dixie-cups of coffee in the morning breathlessly asking each other if they had seen the Quonset hut the night before. Within a week of its first video appearance, Seventh Avenue vendors were selling plastic miniatures of the Quonset hut for $1.98. A previously unknown rock group called Boxer came up with a smash hit called 'Let's Make It in My Quonset Hut.' The song stank but the title became a big favorite in most mid-town bars. Many the Newark commuter didn't make it home that night because he'd gotten lucky with the purring invitation to make it in his Quonset hut.

Johnny Carson came up with one of his few funny monologues in months based on the Quonset hut and Ed McMahon laughed himself silly (which unfortunately convinced the home viewers that the story wasn't so funny after all). Rowan and Martin presented the Wichita Ball Club with the Fickle Finger of Fate Award. Hollywood was already bidding for the rights to a film that had no story (which, on second thought, wasn't that remarkable for Hollywood). A rather sly elder statesman among Washington journalists speculated in his column that the whole business might be the Emperor's New Clothes of the Seventies (but no one paid much serious attention to this famous New Deal newshawk who still referred to African Americans as 'Negroes').

In fairness to the ageing columnist, the Quonset hut was more of a picture spread than a news story. Whenever *Newsweek* or *Time* mentioned the Quonset hut, the written word seemed to vanish from the magazine and page after page of glossy, repetitious, and rather unimaginative photographs appeared in finest National Geographic style.

The wire services weren't doing much better and after a few days their correspondents were simply tacking on a postscript to their homeward bound telexes: 'P.S. The Quonset hut is still there.' One Chicago newspaper ran a black-and-white drawing of the building against a jungle setting on its children's pages and offered a $25 prize for the best crayon or pastel shading. The competition was dropped three days later when the managing editor received an entry wrapped around a large piece of canine excrement.

Supposition. Everything was supposition. The Pentagon refused to make any statement. The White House didn't want to know. The Vice-President had an opinion but discovered no one really cared. A fifth moon landing, which should have been of more significance, was virtually ignored. No one could precisely define the mystique of the Quonset hut but it was fast becoming the Greta Garbo of architecture.

One probably wonders who was making a buck out of all this. Don't be offended. How long did it take after Bobby Kennedy's assassination for posters to go on sale featuring the late senator, his brother, and Dr King against a heavenly background? Who claimed Jimmy Dean's Porsche for salvage and sold tiny bits of it at fifty cents a shot to his heartbroken fans? Spend an afternoon at Whispering Glades or Forest Lawn or whatever the hell it's called. Never to ask for whom the till rings. It rings for thee.

Sales of *Insight* had jumped considerably when the series by David Maxwell had been announced. With his breaking the Quonset hut story and sticking with it, their sales had far exceeded *Time* or *Newsweek*.

David Maxwell *was* the Quonset hut story. The very fact Maxwell had become involved made it a news story. His persistence in following it up daily forced the other media to give it equal attention. Nobody knew what the hell was going on inside the hut but, if anyone could find out, it would be David Maxwell. Everyone firmly believed it. Except for Republican Congresswoman Ethel Kane Kirtsin, who thought the whole thing the biggest hoax perpetrated on America since that ungrateful Wisconsonian George Orson Welles had terrified the radio audience of the republic with his War of the Worlds broadcast. Mrs. Kirtsin would regret to her dying day ever admitting 'that over-sexed, socialist, muckraker' David Maxwell into the country.

Following Maxwell's loaded question at the press briefing and Remington sweating, the man from UPI turned to the man from Reuters and asked a bored: 'What the fuck's going on?'

'Dunno. Somebody woke me up and told me to get the hell over to the briefing. Figured they'd bombed Hanoi.'

'We should be so lucky,' said a photographer from *Life*.

'Belt up, will you?' said the correspondent from *The Times of London*. 'He's not finished.'

Maxwell continued staring at the podium. No sense trying to look into Remington's eyes as they were firmly fixed on the floor. Maxwell concentrated his attention on the captain's moustache. It was the sort Maxwell's Uncle Fred had sported in the RAF. It worked for that war but only made Remington look more of a twit.

'He's not answering you,' whispered PFC Harvey Edelman.

'Good boy. Very observant.'

Remington cleared his throat.

'That's something to take up with the medical officer,' said Remington, hoping he'd lost most of the sentence with his phlegm.

'I've already spoken to Doctor Markson,' replied Maxwell with a contented grin. 'He knows nothing about it.'

'Which clearly reflects how unimportant—'

'Captain! The Wichita Platoon has not been seen for almost a week. On Monday morning a Quonset hut large enough to house the twenty men of the platoon appeared 500 yards outside the base.' (At this point Edelman tugged at the correspondent's sleeve and whispered: '525. I measured it.') Maxwell smiled appreciatively at the St. Louis scribe and continued: 'That same hut is surrounded by a barbed wire fence and twenty armed guards. Could you give us a little more information? Please?'

The other correspondents had been scribbling furiously. It was all news to them. They didn't get around much. Mainly because 85 per cent of them had crabs but were too proud to tell anyone else about it. They spent most of the time in their quarters picking away at their disease. The only writing any of them had done lately was signing tabs in the press club. Now they were working. They hated it.

Burnett Remington began rocking gently. There was nothing religious in his backward and forward swaying. He was no pilgrim at the Wailing Wall. He'd simply lost the use of certain voluntary nerves and knew if he stopped long enough he'd probably shit in his pants. He hadn't done that since he was a child of four in Philadelphia. His mother had given him permission to go trick-or-treating on Hallowe'en for the first time. He hadn't gone but three houses away when he went poopee in his Woody Woodpecker costume. He'd never enjoyed Hallowe'en or Woody Woodpecker since. Remington added this moment to his list of unfavorite memories. Ah! A glimmer of hope. Possibly the swaying motion did not mean that he was going to soil his military trousers. Maybe he was simply going to faint. He prayed to Ayn Rand he'd be able to faint. Remington hardly ever prayed but when he did, he paid tribute to the most positive person he could think of. Burnett thought himself an agnostic but often found that in moments of stress reciting the first few pages of *Atlas Shrugged* could do wonders for him.

Remington had never fainted before. How would he react? Would he enjoy it? Would it become an obsession? Like all those young soldiers who took drugs. Would he become addicted to fainting? Would it become a crutch? Or would things go the other way? Perhaps he'd try so hard to faint that it would result in a stroke that would leave him paralyzed forever. What would happen to his career then? Had he gone to the Point for nothing? Hadn't there been a Remington in the Army since the Spanish-American War? Shame on you, Burnett! Pull yourself together and stop rocking!

He pulled himself together and stopped rocking. Fifteen seconds later he shat his trousers. When he realized what had happened, he collapsed to the floor. It had probably been the worst day in Burnett Remington's life.

The press briefings were cancelled for the next three days while Captain Remington recuperated from his faint in the hospital.

Maxwell continued on with his investigations as best as he could. He had amassed a fantastic list of negative facts but nothing positive. The negatives were tantalizing enough to rate a special report Friday evening (two days after his regular weekly report).

Edelman promised to scour the area of the Quonset hut to come up with some sort of scoop for Maxwell's broadcast. The best he could do were the stubs of Tightass Kelly's middle and index fingers. Maxwell disapproved of atrocities for shock value, so Edelman took great joy in using them for a center-page photo spread in the base paper.

Maxwell went on the air that night calm, understated, yet absolutely in control. Talking about the missing platoon and the appearance of the Quonset hut, the Englishman likened the barbed wire to a spider's web of mystery. He rhetorically asked the fate of the men quarantined in the Quonset hut. Then he answered himself with a quote from his favorite Elizabethan, John Webster: 'We think caged birds sing when, indeed, they cry.'

The reaction in America was electric. No one knew what the hell Maxwell was talking about. His delivery put Gielgud's 'Ages of Man' in the rubbish bin. Maxwell would lose his franchise on the Quonset hut within days, but no one who ever saw his initial Friday night broadcast would ever forget it.


Five days after the broadcast Maxwell sat in his office (Edelman's really, but since the first briefing Harvey was totally devoted to Maxwell and granted him every wish and comfort in his power) staring at a letter.

Edelman arrived with coffee.

'Harvey, what do you think is going on in that Quonset hut?'

'As a journalist or a human being?'

'Helluva distinction,' said Maxwell, sipping his coffee and continuing to stare at the letter.

'You called me Harvey.'

'Not the first time.'

'No. But you're the only person who does. Everyone else calls me Edelman. . .. Am I obnoxious?'

'Honest answer?'

Edelman waited a few seconds: 'Yes.'

'Not basically.'

Immediately after the words left his lips Maxwell could see Edelman entering that all-too easy pose known as Sulk.

'Harvey, play with me you play for keeps. Jimmy Olsen, cub reporter, is out. If anything, it's Hildy Johnson and Walter Burns.'

'Okay... So, what's wrong with me?'

'You've got a lot of hang-ups. Most of them are convenient. The one that blazes brightest in my mind is your labelling anyone anti-Semitic who doesn't like you. Grow up! If I'd spent the last twelve years in punch-ups every time someone took the piss out of my accent, I'd be back in London getting a hunchback over a copy desk. That isn't even the same thing. Here! Suppose you're wearing a pair of black jockey shorts. No one can see them but you. Then you meet some bloke, and you don't hit it off. You don't know why. But being a human being, you need an excuse. You say to yourself it's because you're wearing black jockey shorts. How the hell should he know that?'

'Hey, calm down,' said Edelman, growing a trifle embarrassed at Maxwell's spontaneous demonstration.

'Harvey, I'm trying to help you,' answered Maxwell, noticing that he was breathing harder.

'You shouldn't get involved,' advised Edelman. 'I'm going to see if Captain Remington knows anything. See you later. And take it easy, huh?'

He meant to ask Edelman not to—BANG! Edelman slammed the screen door. It was better he hadn't said anything. Edelman would only have misinterpreted it. Goddam him. Did he have to walk around like the hero of a Bernard Malamud novel? Couldn't he play with himself in finest Philip Roth tradition? Or marry a gentile like any self-respecting Harold Robbins character? Maxwell wouldn't have minded if Harvey had been the one-dimensional cartoon star of a Leon Uris epic. He couldn't carry this flesh-and-blood, basically nice, screwed-up kid from St. Louis, Missouri. On his own, yes. But not with the crabs, Cashbox and Estelle Markson. Here was a letter from Mrs. Roland Alexander Dixon of Detroit, Michigan.


Dear Mr. Maxwell:

Somebody said I should write to you cause you were the man what found out about the Quonset hut.

The reason I am interested is my son Millard Fillmore Dixon is in that Wichita Platoon what is supposed to be held prisoner or sick or something in there.

Millard's a good boy and he didn't go to reform school like his brother Andrew who died from heroin. I didn't ever tell anyone before that Andrew died from heroin. But Millard wrote once or twice and mentioned that you were a clever man and had taught him to speak more refined. Which probably makes you the only person besides me what cared how Millard turned out. Except I don't know any refined words.

Even Millard's Pa didn't know Andrew died of heroin but thinks he died of pnumonia (Spelling?). But now their Pa is dead too so it doesn't much matter.

I didn't want him to go in the army but he joined himself which some folk say was patriotic. But it wasn't that. My son is not a fool. He saw what was happening here and what happened to two of his friends in the riots. He knew it would happen to him to. So he joined up and says they didn't make him.

But I wonder now what is going to happen to him when he comes out. Of the army.

Is he a good baseball player? He is always writing about the team and about the money they are going to win in some big game or other. If he is good enough do you think he could play for Detroit or Cleveland? Does he ever speak to you about this?

I have taken up enough of your time. I wrote mostly to ask you to say hello if you get near that Quonset hut. I haven't heard from Millard in almost a month and I miss him very much. Would you tell him that Florence had her baby? A boy.

I am very proud that my son knows a man as fine and famous as you. And you don't have to tell him about Andrew because I don't think he ever knew.

Thank you.

Mrs. Roland Alexander Dixon


Maxwell hadn't known who Millard Fillmore Dixon was when he first read the letter. Then the 'refined language' bit gave him away. Was he Punjab or the Asp? Didn't really matter. Whoever he was, he was Maxwell's sworn friend. Or so his mother thought. And a guy wouldn't lie to his mother. Dixon really believed Maxwell was his buddy. Why me? What did I ever do except send you up? You and your mate? Why should I share your mother's secret about Andrew? I'm not a private person. Burroughs: 'Whatever is fed to the machine subliminally the machine will eventually process.' You're all grist. You, Harvey Edelman, Milton Markson and all those poor devils in the Quonset hut. Can't be helped. 'My soul like to a ship in a black storm Is driven I know not whither.' I'm not in charge. Just hired help. Understand? Someone else is responsible. I'm a writer. It's my destiny. BOOM!! Ernest Hemingway just stuck a shotgun in his mouth.

The girl had been sitting in the Manhattan office of *Insight* for over four hours oblivious to the information that Adam Frawley, the publisher, was tied up in a very important meeting.

Finally, one of the secretaries asked the girl her name.

Sheila Mendlsohn, she said. Adding *Mrs.* Mendlsohn, as a postscript.

As if she had said the magic password, Sheila Mendlsohn soon found herself zipped up an express elevator, standing in the plush office of Adam Frawley, who was deep in thought by a window-wall commanding a view of Central Park and the north part of the island.

Frawley got up from behind his desk and walked towards Sheila. Tall, well-tailored, grey at the temples. She decided that he was an actor who had been hired to go with the set and play the part of the magazine publisher.

'*Mrs.* Mendlsohn?' Frawley asked, staring at the young girl standing before him. 'I have a daughter your age.'

'And I have a father *your* age,' smiled Sheila.

Frawley laughed and asked her to sit down on the large. Spanish-leather sofa. He offered her a cigarette, then lit it. There was an awkward silence. Then she spoke:

'My husband is Kip Mendlsohn. He's not a ball player or anything. I mean not a professional. It's just that everyone thinks he is. With the name Kip. That or a tennis player . . . I'm sorry. I didn't start this right. You see, I didn't really think I'd get to see you. I'm surprised I saw the secretary. I'm sorry, Mr. Frawley. I'm very nervous.'

'Take your time, Mrs. Mendlsohn. I'm fascinated. You've got me hooked.'

Sheila laughed. She liked Frawley.

'My husband's a member of the Wichita Platoon,' she continued. 'I haven't heard from him in two weeks. We used to write to each other every day. Sometimes we'd send each other tapes. I haven't heard from him in two weeks. I said that didn't I? I still write every day. And the letters must be getting there because they don't send them back to me. Why aren't they letting him write back to me?'

Frawley stared at the girl and saw his own daughter Pam. They were nothing alike. Not physically. But they were the same generation and his heart went out to them. He knew if he allowed himself, he would break his heart every other second of his life. And that would never get a magazine published.

'What I can do for you, Mrs. Mendlsohn?'

'It's about David Maxwell. I went over to the TV studio, but they told me to come over here. I watch Mr. Maxwell every week and read all his *Insight* articles. Everyone does now since this Quonset hut business. Is he a man of integrity?'

'Personal or professional?'

'Is there a difference?'

'How old are you, Sheila?'

'Nineteen.'

'How long have you been married?'

'Fourteen months.'

'And how long has your husband been away?'

'Almost thirteen months. We didn't want to wait. I'd gone with him for almost two years when he was called up.'

'My daughter goes to school in Switzerland. Do you know why?'

'Please, Mr. Frawley. I heard some people talking the other evening. About David Maxwell. They said he was a sensationalist. I'm sorry. I don't know what I want you to tell me.'

Frawley walked over to the window-wall and gazed out. He let himself become part of Manhattan. The anonymity was comforting. He immersed himself in the Waters of Uninvolvement. Switzerland. What could he tell this little girl? Maxwell was officially an employee. Granted one of the highest paid employees in America. Frawley had admired his work for years and had known him casually for eight. Cocktail parties, fund-raising dinners, a wave across a restaurant. Who the hell knew him? Maybe Audrey.

The taxi dropped Sheila off in front of a townhouse in the East Sixties. She rang the bell and was shown upstairs to a warm, wood-paneled, thick-carpeted study adorned with Tiffany lamps and nineteenth-century prints.

Sheila wandered about the room until she heard someone come in behind her.

A short vivacious woman in her late thirties stood before her and held her hand out warmly.

'I'm Audrey Maxwell.'

Sheila rapped with her for hours about men, clothes, hairstyles, books, films, and grass. Their twenty-year age difference didn't matter. Audrey looked so young and reminded Sheila of her section head at a summer camp where she had been a counsellor.

It was evening when Sheila removed the cassette from her purse. It was the last tape that Kip had sent her the night before the Wichita Platoon had gone on its mission.

Audrey closed the study door and placed the cartridge in the tape recorder. A male, New York voice in its early twenties came out of the machine:

'How are ya? I'm recording this in the can cuz there's nowhere else to get any privacy in this goddam place. I guess it isn't the most romantic place in the world to talk to your wife. Sitting in cubicle three in an oriental latrine. But let's pretend it's the Adirondacks. Right? I miss you, Sheila. I know I said I wasn't going to go on about that in these tapes but what's the sense of bullshitting. It's gone past the stage of being horny. It's becoming a kind of religion now. Thinking about getting out of here and back to you. We keep hearing about overkill out here. I wonder if there's something like emotional overkill. Waiting so long to see someone and then finding out that you killed the nerves because of so much effort. . . . Oh, wow! I think I'm going to start tripping again. Ha-ha-ha. Excuse me. . . . Last night we were lying around after lights out and we started rapping about old records. You know like Jailhouse Rock, Diana, the Flying Purple People Eater whatever the hell it was. Fats Domino and Chubby Checker. And we started remembering like when Buddy Holly and the Big Bopper died in that plane crash. That was ten years ago. More, I think. You know. And then it hit me I can remember ten years ago. And like reminisce. Nostalgia! It's kind of scary. You know you sit and you hear your folks talk about the war and the ration books and the victory gardens. And it sounds so ancient. And you never think that it'll ever apply to you. But I met a kid last week from Pittsburgh. He was about 17. He never heard of Dinah Shore. How the hell couldn't he have heard of Dinah Shore? Doesn't he remember the big MWAH every Sunday night on television? And Pinky Lee. Who the hell's Pinky Lee? he asked me. I didn't dare ask him about Howdy Doody and Mr. Bluster. I mean if he didn't know them then I'd be convinced this war was a big mistake. . . . Oh, yeah. We almost got into another fight tonight with those goddam fascist Montana Cowboys. They're really sick you know. Bunch of fucking Nazis. They were sitting there arguing how many villages they'd destroyed. Who the hell made this a competition? . . . . Cleet Fowler. Thinks he's Wyatt Earp. To tell you the truth I'm not so excited now about this ball game with them. Fowler figures he's Spartacus or something. Sitting there telling his buddies about the parts of the body that are wounds, slow deaths, and instant kills. I mean, what is that? Christ! I want to get out of here. Thank God for getting smashed. If we didn't have grass I think I'd go out of my mind. I really feel like an idiot now when I remember that party we went to and that guy from Cornell offered us a joint. We must have looked like a couple of Mormons or something. "Oh, no! We never touch it!" Wow. I wish to God they'd legalize the stuff. That's why I don't want you smoking till I get back. With your luck, you'd get busted the first time. And Edelman would pick the story up for sure. I don't know how but that little shmuck finds out everything that's going on. WICHITA BALLPLAYER'S WIFE ARRESTED ON DRUGS CHARGE. My mother would get the marriage annulled long distance. Yeah, I guess she's in the Holy Land by now. Miami Beach. Three wise men coming out of the pool. ZAP! Hi, Jesus. What do you want for your birthday little fellow?' (At this point a voice could be heard in the background shouting: 'Can you keep the noise down in the recording studio?') Oops. I think I'm getting a little loud. I don't know what the hell they're complaining about. Kaplan keeps his records going full blast day and night. I've got Janis Joplin for a roommate. Her and her bottle of bourbon, poor broad. We don't drink anymore in here—by the way. Which should keep my mother happy. 'What do you have to drink for anyhow? Are you an insurance salesman? My brother Bill was an insurance salesman and look what happened to him.' As I recall him my Uncle Bill was a sharp-looking guy who used to get laid a lot on the road. He dropped dead in a motel in Syracuse. How the hell did I get on to my Uncle Bill? Oh, yeah. Listen. Before I forget. Remember that guy from Shaker Heights that your cousin wanted me to look up? In the air-cavalry unit? He's dead. Jeese, I felt stupid. I drove over to where he was stationed one afternoon last week. Tommy and I borrowed a jeep. We gave some stupid story. And we drove to this village about half an hour away. We jumped out of the jeep, you know. And we went up to this sergeant and asked him if he knew Bruce Fletcher. Then this jerk just stared at us for about two minutes then pointed towards a truck where they were loading a coffin. Helicopter crash. I don't know what you're going to tell your cousin. I hope she wasn't going with him or anything. . . . Hold on a second. Somebody has to take a pee. . . . Okay. I don't know what else to say. Everybody's still kidding Ramirez about the grapes. You remember Ramirez? Our second baseman who doesn't speak English so good. Poor bastard. He volunteered to get his immigration papers through quicker. He's not a bad second baseman. And he's teaching some of us to speak Spanish. Except I think it's bastard Spanish. You know, Mexican. . . . I wish just once when I record these things that something screwy would happen to the machine and I'd suddenly hear you answering me at the same time instead of waiting a week. I guess it would be impossible to book a phone call over here and it'd probably cost a fortune anyhow. But I don't care. It's just that I can never figure out the time difference. When you'd be at class. I had a dream last week where I called the operator and asked her what time it was in New York and she said: 'Never.' Wow. I've been having some weird dreams lately. I mean the kind your crazy cousin Sidney could write a book about. Remember that girl Cashbox I told you about? I guess she's kind of like a prostitute. I don't know. Probably not. You know the way guys talk out here. Every Oriental chick's a hooker to them. Ah. forget it. I don't know what I brought it up for. Hey, listen! I don't want you to get the idea there's anything going on between me and her. I'm not going to lie to you and say I haven't had the occasional erotic dream about her. I mean you should see her. You'd understand. But I couldn't afford her. Even if I *really* wanted to. I mean she's a hundred dollars a shot. Or so they say. . . . Listen, I know it's a crazy time to bring it up but where do you want to go when I get home? The first night, I mean. Tommy and I and a bunch of the guys thought of renting Arthur for the night. I know it sounds crazy. But apparently, Tommy's old man is loaded and he could—Hold on a second! . . . . I have to go now. Keller just came in and told us we're going on a mission in the morning. Just one of those search-and-destroy things where nothing ever happens. Probably be back tomorrow night. Saturday night. I don't know how the hell you're holding out but if I talk dirty on this tape I'm told the post office won't deliver it. Sheila, I love you. I love you, I love you, I love you. Goodbye.'

There was a silence before Audrey leaned forward and turned off the tape recorder.

'I like him,' she said to Sheila.

'Thank you.'

'Hungry?'

'Mmm. Yes.'

'I'll get Holly to bring us some sandwiches.'

A light snow started to fall on 68th Street. Audrey got the logs going in the fireplace, poured herself a brandy, put her feet up, and settled into a green leather high-backed chair to talk about Maxwell.

'I don't know why we got divorced. Probably because we didn't have any children. Not that that was the cause but it would have been the only reason for us to stick together. We just never seemed to be at the same place at the same time. Not once David became famous . . . But the early years were great fun. He was possessed of the most remarkable pin for bursting hot air balloons. My mother stopped inviting him to dinner parties. All her finishing school chums sitting around over vichyssoise trying to impress David with quotations from Shakespeare. He hates Shakespeare. Has no admiration for him whatsoever. Calls him a punchboard success. He felt that if anyone wrote that many plays, he was bound to come up with a few winners. No. He's a great fan of the underdog. He absolutely adored Webster. "Two plays. Two hits." It was Webster who got him banished from my mother's dining room. There was a lull one evening during the soup sipping and David let loose with: "Women are caught as you take tortoises. She must be turned on her back." God, he was bloody marvelous.'

'Has he changed?' asked Sheila innocently.

'I don't think so. We still go out sometimes. And if we're in the same place at Christmas we spend it together. But with the NASA thing and the war I haven't seen him for almost a year.'

'But what about the broadcasts?' asked Sheila, pressing for an answer.

'I have seen him put his hand into a top hat with no false bottom and I have seen him pull an honest-to-God rabbit out of it. He's not sticking with that Quonset hut for kicks. Whether he knows what's going on in there and won't tell because he wants to milk it as long as possible, I'm not sure. But I doubt it. No one loves a scoop better than David and he'd never sit on a story this long.'

Two hours later Audrey rang for a cab and sent Sheila back downtown to the NYU girls' dormitory. She smoked three cigarettes and phoned Adam Frawley at home. After Frawley gave her a long complicated overseas number, Audrey booked the call and went to bed.

Ring! Ring! Ring!

'Hello.'

'Hello, my ownest own.'

'Audrey! Are you out of your mind? Why are you ringing me in Saigon?'

'I wanted to talk to you.'

'You must be mad. This phone call costs more than the war. Who's paying for this?'

'You are.'

'You rang collect?'

'No, darling, it's coming out of the alimony. Which I only took as a tax dodge for you. So lay off. What's the matter with you, David?'

'Nothing.'

'Has the magic gone out of our marriage?'

'The marriage has gone out of our marriage. We're divorced.'

'I just spent the saddest evening with a little girl named Sheila Mendlsohn. Her husband is in the Wichita Platoon.'

'So?'

'What do you mean 'so', you callous bastard?'

'Audrey, suppose I said I couldn't talk to you now?'

'You mean the phone's tapped?'

'Possibly,' said Maxwell letting out a deep breath.

'Oh, listen,' Audrey laughed. 'Before I forget, is there really a girl out there named Cashbox?'

'Who told you? Look, Audrey, we are legally divorced and any—'

'Ooooh!'

'What is that? Your Frankie Howerd imitation? What are you doing?'

'Listen, darling, alimony or no alimony, this phone call is getting out of hand. Tell me what's happening in that Quonset hut for that little girl's sake.'

'Remember what I always talked about?' asked Maxwell. 'My dream?'

'You mean *the* story? Is this it?'

'I think so. But someone's moving heaven and earth to keep me from getting it.'

'Are you going to get it?'

'What do you think?'

There was a slight pause on the American end of the line then: 'David Maxwell, you're a goddam wonderful man and I still love you.' She hung up.

Adam Frawley hadn't been able to get to sleep that night and finally reached Maxwell on the phone after a two-hour delay.

'What? Are you and my wife on retainers from Bell Telephone? Trying to get the stock up?'

Frawley explained his concern over the quarantine story and his belief if Sheila Mendlsohn doubted its validity there might be thousands—possibly millions—of Americans who felt the same way. Maxwell assured Frawley—wiretap or no wiretap—there was no quarantine. If the publisher wanted, Maxwell would get a sworn statement to that effect from Dr. Markson, the chief medical officer. Frawley liked the statement idea so much he decided to reproduce the document on the next cover of *Insight*.

Maxwell walked into the infirmary a few minutes later. He encountered a doctor he'd never seen before and a host of nurses who all looked different. None of them giggled when he walked in that day as opposed to the regular nurses who had had great fun at the expense of his disease. Not even a titter with this new crowd.

'Can you tell me where Dr. Markson is?'

'Who?'

'Milton Markson, the chief medical officer,' explained Maxwell, convinced now that *all* doctors were idiots.

'Sorry. There's no Doctor Markson here.'

'I think you're mistaken.'

'Don't think so. *I'm* the chief medical officer here. My name is Renfrew.'

'Dr. Renfrew, I don't know what sort of game is going on here, but for five months I have been treated almost daily by Milton Markson in that office!'

Renfrew politely held his hand out for Maxwell to go into the office and have a look.

It was the same office, all right, but where was the picture of Milton Markson with the Tufts Basketball team? Where was the crocheted allegiance to the flag that Estelle had spent so many hours on? When had Dr. Renfrew's name appeared on the door?

'Markson's assistant, that kid, Collins. Where is he?'

'There's no Dr. Collins here.'

'And my nurses? Where are my lovely idiotic nurses?'

'I don't think that's any way to speak about the staff.' said Renfrew. 'Help is so difficult to come by these days.'

Maxwell glared briefly at Renfrew, then stormed out of the Infirmary. He headed straight for Markson's quarters where he had played cribbage with him one evening and knocked at the door. No answer. Maxwell opened the door and found the flat spotless and empty. Nothing; no furniture; no clothes; no visible signs of life.

Within an hour it became clear to Maxwell that Milton Markson and his entire staff had vanished from the face of the earth and with them had gone *the* story.

# THE MURDER MAN

Will you stop making a fool of yourself? It's not the sort of thing Clarence Darrow would have sweated over. You're concerned with jurisprudence. Not selling vodka or button-down shirts. Get an eye-patch. Fight a war. You *fought* a war. Almost. Wasn't your fault they didn't send you overseas. If you had gone overseas, you'd only have gotten yourself killed. Right? If you'd gotten yourself bumped off, you'd never have met Rochelle. Darling Rocky. Just what you needed! Going off on a Kramer trip. Pretty soon Malka's inanities will come creeping through your cranium. Any minute now you'll come to realize the thoughts you thought you were thinking strictly to yourself have been coming very slowly out of your lips and everyone in the elevator will have heard them. Except there's no one else in the elevator so you might as well talk to yourself.

'Thank God. If I shut my mouth for another second, I'd have gone crazy. Mmmm! Voice sounds good today. La-la-la-laaaa! Oh, yes. God! What I need is a case! A real ball breaker. Maybe a civil rights job, with a first-class bigot presiding. Yeah. Run him a while with the old Wyoming folksiness. Let the voice go a bit. Then bang down on his ass with the scales of justice and a couple of low notes—'

Graham had failed to notice the elevator stopping on the twelfth floor and a brunette secretary from Bochner's office stepping into the car with him. She stared at him.

He noticed her stare in the corner of his eye but he did not blush, stammer, or make an excuse. He simply drew in air. A huge gust of air which added another half foot to his six-foot frame. He turned his head slowly, calculatingly to the young girl, and gave her the fullness of his blue eyes.

'Good morning,' he said.

God! that sounded good, he thought to himself. What a good morning! What balls! The sort of good morning D. H. Lawrence would have wished *he'd* said. How does that grab you, little girl? Get you deep down in your panties? Probably go home at lunch time and change. Or maybe you carry a spare pair with you in case I say good morning in the elevator. Who could blame you, doll? How can you beat that voice? They wouldn't let me talk till I was sixteen. Afraid I'd get arrested.

'Oh, hello, Mr. Graham. Talking to yourself again?'

Stupid little bitch got out of the elevator the floor before Graham's so he didn't have to worry about her getting the last exit. That's all he'd need. Stupid idiot broad from Bochner's office getting the last exit. Bochner *would* hire a mental defective like that. What the hell did Bochner know? With that whining, nasal, sing-song voice of his. Which is why Bochner never went into court. Bullshit, he found more excitement in the office. Bochner didn't have the voice. Couldn't make the music. Couldn't make the jury one. An emotional sponge he could ring out at his every whim and not have it go dry on him.

Doors open. The Murder Man walks assuredly down the corridor to his office. Where'll they put the camera, Graham thought to himself? Maybe one of those great track shots with the camera on the floor shooting up at him. Then the voice-over: 'I'm Frank Graham. I'm a lawyer. They call me the Murder Man.' Beautiful. Beautiful. Fan-fucking-tastic! Why did radio have to die? I could have been Sam Spade or Marlowe. One of those guys. Ah, what's the use of talking? I can't even get on the Johnny Carson show. There I go again. Ego, ego, ego. I'm a humanitarian not a film star. I save people's lives. People who no one else wants to save. I saved Roland Rizitski when no one else would touch him. Whoopee! Want a medal now or later?

I don't want to enter through the front door today, Graham thought to himself as he confronted the simple FRANK GRAHAM, Attorney-at-law, which faced him. Encountering all those clawing, begging, whimpering, forlorn, hopeless, helpless, hapless victims of society. God! Why doesn't the world sanction talking to yourself? I just wasted the greatest speech on my mind.

Graham took out the key to his inner office and opened the door. He had been worried for a second it was his birthday, and he would be greeted by an obnoxious chorus of 'surprise, surprise'. But no one was there. They had forgotten. He remembered that it wasn't his birthday for another seven months. Graham wasn't *that* anxious to turn forty. Not without winning *the* case. But lately, he had resigned himself to not getting anywhere near *the* case until he was sixty. After all, Darrow wasn't a youngster when he defended Leopold and Loeb. Or when he clobbered Jennings Bryan. But Darrow didn't do the movie either. Tracy and Welles got all the glory for that. Graham knew he had a better voice than Tracy's. Welles was another story. But Welles had had the radio. No. If Graham found *the* case while he was still reasonably young there was a chance—a slight one—but still a chance that he might be able to play himself in the movie. He was positive he could con Preminger into it. The face was no problem. Not since Burton had made pock marks popular. Fifteen years ago, no one would have looked at Frank Graham with those holes in his face. Until *Cleopatra*. Graham would be eternally grateful to Elizabeth Taylor. Or was it Richard Burton? Probably both. They had made him a star. Oh, he'd always had the voice. Now the face had caught up with it. Suddenly the papers were running *his* picture alongside the ample proportions of his stunning mass murderesses. He'd even been invited on to a few Sunday afternoon public affairs shows. But not Johnny Carson. What does he expect me to do? Call him up and beg? Maybe I should get a press agent? No, that's ridiculous. Bad for the image. What a waste! I could tell him all about my boyhood in Wyoming. Tell them the whole truth about the Rizitsky case. Bochner says I should write a book. The man is sick. They'll never hear my voice in a book. I hope Carson kills someone. *Then* let him try and phone me.

The Murder Man sat down at his desk and stared at that morning's New York Times. Goddam war. It's costing a fortune. Pushed Howie's case— Graham began rifling through the first section—Page seven! Raping a blind girl goes on page seven these days? How the hell is anyone supposed to get any work? Mind you, she wasn't really blind. Graham's colleague had merely said that to gain some badly needed sympathy for his short-sighted client who was a bit of a slut from White Plains. Graham advised the man not to take the case. But what was one supposed to do in the off-season? What with the recession and everything.

It wasn't that Graham hadn't wanted to work those last five months. But how was he supposed to outdo the Clapham case? It had lasted four months, gone through three juries and one dead judge. Go figure old man Pankris would just heave out like that in the middle of the case? In the middle of one of Graham's speeches! That had been a hard one, too.

The Murder Man, while a hell of a speaker and one of the nimblest legal minds to ever nijinski an unbought jury, didn't have the greatest natural command of the language. He blamed these occasional lapses from intelligible English to his East European-born parents, who emigrated to America just before the First World War and settled for some unknown reason in the state of Wyoming. Add to this the fact that his ex-wife, Rochelle Kramer Easterbrooke Graham, was from an annually Jewish family and one can well estimate the Murder Man's excuses for an occasional slip from syntax. What Graham needed was a writer. Someone who could be handed the strategy of the case and then adorn that winning procedure with the proper literary bon mots, quotes, profound, and, more importantly, quotable thoughts.

Graham's eyes returned once more to the front page where he could admire an article about a master of words. Graham didn't mind being referred to as 'the David Maxwell of the courtroom' for he revered the Englishman's writing and many times wished he could hire Maxwell to write one of his cases. But the man couldn't be bought. Ah! but to collaborate on a case was something to be kept in mind for the future. Now what had the Pulitzer Prize-winning author of mid-Atlantis gotten himself into?

**Saigon—The army today verified and presented documents to attest to the quarantine of the Wichita Platoon.**

**This was much in protest to the theory launched by prize-winning author David Maxwell that no quarantine existed.**

**More importantly Maxwell has charged that the base's chief medical officer, Milton Markson, was abducted with the rest of SEE PAGE NINETEEN: MAXWELL**

Graham noted a special bulletin box at the bottom of the page.

> **BULLETIN: The Pentagon claimed on Tuesday that there is no Milton Markson in the armed forces. A further check with the American. Medical Association revealed that there is no Dr Markson among their numbers either.**

Graham shook his head sadly. Maxwell had finally overstepped the bounds of accurate journalism and tumbled foolishly into pulp fiction.

The Murder Man's attention was diverted to a list of telephone messages that he had received that morning. He reached instinctively for the intercom and buzzed Mrs. Proctor.

'Yes, Mr. Graham?' asked a strange voice.

'Who's that?'

'Miss Cable from Office Overload.'

'Where's Mrs. Proctor? Who are these messages from? Mrs. Proctor reads Dunn and Bradstreet, the Social Register, Variety.'

'Sorry, sir, she's gone on holiday and the agency sent me.'

'Oh, all right. Speak to you later.'

The lawyer was angry with himself for letting his voice get out of control. Miss Cable would get the wrong idea from that wavering delivery on the intercom. He buzzed the outer office again.

'Miss Cable, get in here,' he said in his best basso.

Miss Cable walked in. Graham fought desperately to keep his cool. Mrs. Proctor was 52 years old and a happy grandmother. Miss Cable was 22 and built like a brick shithouse. A definite threat to Graham's working and staying power.

'This is a law office. We practice law here. Law is practiced here. This is where it happens. Law is my thing. I like doing my thing. Nothing must impede the execution of my thing. My thing being the law. This is a law office.'

Miss Cable was panting for breath. That voice. It was like a hand thrust down one's tights. That voice had come out of the man in front of her. That same fantastic voice that had spoken to her the second time from the box. She had thought there were two men in there. The first sound had been so gay and wimpy but this voice matched the man, this fantastic-looking man.

Oh, shit, Graham said to himself. Gave her too much voice. Went straight to her snatch. Stupid girl. The voice is meant for the heart not the snatch. The heart and the brain. He'd have to get rid of this girl. Send her downstairs to Bochner.

Sensing the imminence of banishment, the girl quickly piped up with: 'I'm glad you set that straight for me, Mr. Graham. I'll try and be worthy of that ideal for the short time I'll be here.'

Not so dumb, he thought after she left. Knows how to beg without asking. Ambitious, too. Note the clever phraseology of 'the short time I'll be here'. Clever. She hopes for the future. Mmm. Maybe she might work out after all. Possible journeywoman to write his cases. Wonder if she's read any Shakespeare. How could I explain her to Mrs. Proctor? Negates the whole purpose of engaging Mrs. Proctor. The grandmother was hired for the very fact she was a grandmother. Placid soul, happy home life, intelligent mother-manageress. The last person on earth whose ass he'd want to sink his teeth into. Miss Cable's derriere was a different story altogether.

He looked instinctively towards the photograph of Rochelle and the two kids. That was a big con. He'd been divorced from Rocky for almost two years. Six months ago, he'd finally forgiven Bochner for handling his wife's divorce. Damn whining, nasal, sing-song voice.

He'd never figured out whether Malka had been satisfied at the outcome or not. And why not? She'd engineered the disintegration of the marriage as easily as she had arranged the conception of the relationship.

In 1957 after winning several law prizes and writing a published thesis on criminal law Graham took up an offer to lecture at Columbia University. The work was all right but not what Graham really wanted. Not what he knew in his soul he was meant to do: to speak in a courtroom. Be a conjurer of words tossing phrases haphazardly into the air and have them fall neatly to the ground spelling out the allegiance to the flag to the amazement and admiration of all.

Those days were still ahead of him as he stared out at the thirty-five drowsy, well-dressed, young men in his class at Columbia Law School. None ever bothered with the assigned readings from the previous night. Each one chose a different paragraph and when things got tense, they could always question Graham about the complexity of those few sentences and make it look as if they'd tackled the whole assignment. Graham wanted to walk out more than once but decided to sublimate and squelch any bravura performances until such time as he had the biggest possible and most appreciative audience. When? When?

One day he noticed Eric. Eric had no text, notebook, or pencil but he was more attentive and interested than the other thirty-five cretins put together. He also appeared to be much younger than any of the others in the class. Ridiculously younger. He couldn't be more than eighteen. And he wasn't. He wasn't even enrolled. Graham discovered the boy was a dropout piano prodigy who thought he might be interested in criminal law and started sitting in on Graham's classes. Graham didn't mind but thought it ironic that the person who most cared about his lectures wasn't even a student.

Having attended Graham's classes for three weeks, Eric approached the lawyer at the end of a session.

Eric's mother had a case, (Graham was later to realize that Eric's mother *was* a case) and believed Mr. Graham was the only person in the greater New York area who could handle it. Eric and the lawyer barreled into the latter's Volkswagen at the end of the day and drove to Forest Hills.

Graham was met at the door by Malka Kramer, a 45-year-old Austrian refugee whose erratic behavior Eric embarrassedly attributed to menopause. (Frank later found out from Rochelle that her mother's menopause had been going on for at least ten years.)

'Mr. Graham?' Malka squealed in her excitable Viennese manner. 'Eric has told me so much about you. Such a wicked boy, Eric. But I knew he wasn't lying about you.'

Eric sifted through the mail on the hallway table and discovered all his letters had been opened.

'Mother, did you open my mail?'

'What? What is it you are asking me?' flustered Malka. 'Such a wicked boy, Eric! Can't you see I am talking to Mr. Graham?'

'Mother, you've been reading my mail again.'

'And why not? How else is a mother supposed to find out what her sons are doing? Don't you think so, Mr. Graham? I used to read all of Gary's letters in his drawer. Did you know that my Gary lost his virginity when he was fifteen? He is even more wicked than Eric. Oh! Eric is pouting again. Eric always pouts in front of his mama.'

Graham was a little embarrassed by the intimacy he'd been exposed to. And who was Gary? Never mind. What about the case?

'About your case, Mrs. Kramer?'

'We have lots of time to talk about that. Come into the living room and relax. Would you like something to drink?'

Graham walked down three steps into a warm. wooden-beamed room. French windows let out into a garden. Standing by the windows was a stunning. blonde-haired girl in her mid-twenties.

'Oooh!' gushed Malka. 'I didn't know you were in here, darling. This is my daughter Rochelle. Rochelle, this is Eric's friend, Mr. Graham, who teaches at the law school.'

Graham heard Eric moan from the hallway.

'Would you two excuse me for a minute?' asked Malka, who exited to the hallway and maneuvered Eric into the colonial kitchen.

'What is the matter wiz you?' she asked, quite annoyed.

'When did Rocky come home?' asked Eric. 'I thought she was still in San Francisco.'

'You are such a wicked boy, Eric! Since when is it a crime for a girl to want to visit her family? Aren't you glad to see your sister?'

'That's not what I'm talking about. Isn't it a little more than coincidence my bringing Mr. Graham home and finding Rocky here after three months?'

'Please, Eric, I'm getting a headache. You know I'm not well and it's wicked of you to go on like this. No one else treats their mother like this. You should be ashamed. Go upstairs and read your letters and I'll call you when supper is ready.'

Malka returned to the living room a few minutes later to find Graham and her daughter getting along famously. Rochelle worked for an advertising company in San Francisco and the lawyer was reminiscing about his postgraduate work at Berkely. Malka smiled and contributed the occasional inanity to the conversation.

The trio was joined a few minutes later by an exuberant 12-year-old girl—a miniature of Rochelle. This was Melissa, the youngest member of the Kramer family.

'Bobby Hertzberg wants to marry me,' said Melissa, stretching herself out full-length on the floor in front of the fireplace and assuming various ballet postures. 'But I think he's far too immature for me. He still reads the "Hardy Boys". I mean, can you get excited over *The Tower Treasure*?' She threw herself forward and leaned on Graham's knees. 'Mother won't let me wear a brassiere yet. How am I supposed to think about love and not be able to wear a brassiere? Think what will happen to me. I'll be forty with big floppy breasts like Aunt Esther in Montreal. Ooh! Sometimes I think you hate me, Mother.'

'Come and kiss me,' giggled Malka. Melissa did as her mother asked. 'You know I told you how a brassiere is an encumbrance on a woman's soul. Part of your heart is lost forever the day you snap on your first bra. Don't you think so, Mr. Graham?'

How the hell should I know, Graham asked himself. You're nuts, lady. Your whole family. Except for your beautiful daughter, who is sitting far too far away from me on this sofa. What are you thinking beautiful blonde lady? Would you like me to take you out of this madhouse?

Rochelle could not read Graham's thoughts. Even if she could she'd have been interrupted by her mother's insistence the lawyer stay to dinner. There was a huge roast in the oven which no one would eat if he didn't join them.

'Eric, go upstairs and tell your father we'll be eating soon.'

'Is your husband not well?' asked Graham for the inane reason he couldn't imagine why her husband would be upstairs at this early hour.

'Oh, no. He has a studio in the attic.'

'He's an artist?'

'No. No. He just likes to . . .' Malka smiled and made some vague gesture with her hands.

Paul Kramer, a cherubic, grey-haired man, wearing glasses and a polite smile, came down the stairs a few minutes later. He had a slight Austrian accent not as pronounced as his wife.

Supper, or as Graham later came to refer to it: The Malka Kramer Show, was reasonably pleasant. Eric no longer said anything to Graham (he had been so gregarious on the drive to Queens); Melissa feigned food poisoning on three different occasions; Paul ate with a distant but contented look; Rochelle, thought Graham, had touched his leg once under the table (but then it could easily have been Malka or Melissa). And Malka talked. Graham would ask other members of the family questions and Malka would answer for them.

Through his self-appointed interpreter, Graham learned that Rochelle shared an apartment in San Francisco with Gary, her folk singing brother; Melissa wanted to be a ballerina but would be happily married instead by the time she was twenty. (Graham wondered how Rochelle had missed 'being happily married by the time she was twenty'); Eric had abandoned a great future as a concert pianist, dropped out of everything, and was occasionally playing jazz in the village at weekends. Graham also noticed Paul and Eric occasionally gazing at each other during the meal and smiling warmly. This made the lawyer feel that there was possibly some hope for the family.

The telephone rang.

'It's Gary! Gary!' screamed Melissa, with enough volume everyone at Idlewild Airport could hear her.

There was a mass exodus from the dinner table and Graham felt a little dumb being left there alone. But it wasn't *his* brother on the telephone, so there was no reason to join the others.

Rochelle got on the phone first and giggled for about two minutes. Paul said some nice fatherly things. Melissa grabbed the phone away from her father and started crying about the fact her mother wouldn't let her wear a brassiere. Eric didn't want to speak to his brother. Malka got on the extension in her bedroom and told Gary what a wicked boy he was.

'Come talk to Gary!' Melissa shouted at Graham. The lawyer smiled. Malka's voice shouted down from upstairs: 'Yes, give the phone to Mr. Graham.'

Melissa dragged Graham into the breakfast room where her father, brother, and sister were gathered round the wall telephone. The receiver was thrust into the lawyer's hand.

'Hello,' said Graham.

'Hi,' said the cheerful, boyish voice on the other end.

'I'm Frank Graham,' said Graham for want of anything better to say.

'Good luck.'

'Pardon?'

'Good luck.' Gary hung up.

Strange family, Graham thought to himself.

As the family returned to the dining room for coffee Mr. Kramer cornered Graham. The former had not said a word to his guest during the meal.

'Is that your Volkswagen out there?' asked Paul.

'Yes.'

Mr. Kramer nodded his head gravely and climbed up the stairs to his studio.

By the time Graham returned to the dining room he discovered that Eric had vanished, Melissa had gone to visit a girlfriend and Malka had been struck down by a migraine. He was alone with Rochelle on the sofa.

'Are you doing anything this evening?' he asked.

'No,' she answered noncommittally. After a slight pause, she moved closer to him and touched the baby finger of his right hand with the baby finger of her left hand.

'Don't say anything about them,' she said.

Graham turned his face towards her. He didn't really want to kiss her. Not the way he had *wanted* to kiss her earlier. But the kiss grew until it was all.

'Are we going to get married?' she asked looking up at him.

Graham stared at her.

'I'm only joking.' she laughed, then added: 'Half.'

Graham became a regular addition to the Kramer household for the next few months. After Rochelle subtly advised him to trade his Volkswagen in for a second-hand Ford, her father became much friendlier towards the lawyer. Eric stayed away from the house for long periods of time and Melissa was as zany as ever.

'I like you much better than Marty,' the youngest daughter said to the lawyer one day.

'Who's Marty?'

'Rocky's first husband.'

Subtle, very subtle. Graham should have taken that bit of information as the first warning and gotten the hell out of there, but it was still early in his relationship with Rochelle. If she hadn't wanted to tell him she'd been married before, she must have had her reasons. When he did ask her she informed him that she had been married to Dr Martin Easterbrook for half a year and the whole thing simply hadn't worked. Simple enough. It satisfied Graham.

Until he had coffee with Malka, who graphically discussed her daughter's sexual relationships with her ex-husband.

'How do you know all this?' asked Graham, half fascinated, half-appalled.

'A mother knows,' smiled Malka. 'I made her tell me everything. He was such a disappointment that Marty. I thought I'd made such a good choice.'

Second warning. Ignored again. Malka's 'choice'. The divine Kramer plan. Graham came to realize Eric had honestly wandered into his classroom for the acquisition of knowledge. His fatal mistake was telling his mother about Graham. And Malka, who had already screwed up her daughter's first marriage, sought to make amends by fixing her up with this young legal wizard. Eric realized too late the role he had played in his mother's plot and stayed away from Graham ever after out of embarrassment.

It wasn't until two children and a divorce later that Graham realized all these things were true. Malka had sought to further her future son-in-law's career in those early days. She was the one who convinced him to give up teaching and go into private practice on his own. For the first three months after his marriage, Malka subsidized his far-from-healthy income. She was marvelous the first year-and-a-half of their marriage. He and Rocky were very happy. When Malka read about Roland Rizitski in the newspaper, she convinced Graham this was his big break.

Roland Rizitski was a butcher on Delancey Street, who had murdered his wife in front of seven witnesses. There wasn't a lawyer in the five boroughs who'd handle his case. Graham not only took the case but with a not guilty plea. Everyone thought he was crazy. After two weeks of bullshitting in the courtroom, even Graham thought himself crazy.

He and Rochelle got stoned at a party one night. Graham didn't think anything would happen. At best it would be like getting drunk. The experience wasn't anything he'd anticipated. It was fantastic. Touch, sense, smell. Everything was heightened. Rocky wasn't enjoying it at all. She became paranoid and started weeping uncontrollably. Unable to calm her down, Graham had one of the old pros call a cab. The lawyer was so stoned he couldn't get through the dialing and take them home.

By the time he finally got Rochelle to sleep, Graham had come down sufficiently to do some serious, constructive thinking. That was when the defense came to him. It was a long shot but, if his suspicions and hopes were right, he could spring Roland Rizitski. It would mean hiring a string of investigators at a considerable expense, but it was the risk he had to take. He would have to get his voice out of moth balls. The voice he hadn't used since college when he played Othello and won the debating cup. The voice was two-thirds there but not the way he wanted it for the courtroom.

Graham called for a week's adjournment. When the seven days had lapsed, he returned to the downtown courthouse and made legal history.

He proved that all seven witnesses had taken drugs at one time or another and by summoning various medical experts claimed that the seven people had all been 'tripping' at the time of the 'alleged' murder and had all imagined they'd seen the same thing. Graham's voice was hypnotic as he demanded the judge rule their testimonies invalid. The judge, who was a bit senile and facing an election, was bowled over by the Wyoming defense counsel, adjourned the case, and attributed Mrs. Rizitski's death to unknown causes despite the coroner's detailed report. The legend of the Murder Man had begun. No one paid much attention when eleven months later Roland Rizitski hanged himself in a Palm Beach hotel room.

Graham found himself inundated with retainers and requests from wealthy clients. Rocky was expecting their first child. Graham was a success. And Malka's midnight phone calls began.

They had seemed harmless at first. Just Mother worrying if her daughter was all right and eating enough in those important months. After Stuart was born, she started calling later. Sometimes at three in the morning. Rocky could never get back to sleep after those calls and she never told Graham what her mother had said.

Malka's 'menopause' grew worse, and she insisted Rochelle accompany her on recuperative trips. Quite often these trips coincided with a case that Graham was working on and he was glad to have Rocky away so that he wouldn't be irritable and tense in front of her. There were times though when Graham needed her desperately and she was always off with her mother.

When little Gabrielle was born and Graham left a month later to handle a case in Seattle, Rochelle took the children and moved back to Forest Hills with her mother.

A triumphant Graham returned from Seattle to discover Rochelle wanted a divorce.

'Are you joking?' Graham asked.

'You don't love me, Frank. You're in love with murder.'

'What does that mean?' Graham demanded. 'Do you know what you're saying? Wait a minute. Just wait a minute. What kind of poison has your mother been putting in your mind?'

'My mother has nothing to do with it.'

'Bullshit. She's a sick woman who's delighted in destroying her children's lives these past thirty years. Why did Gary leave home? Why is Eric so messed up? Why does your father lock himself up in the attic all the time? He gave up long ago. What was the matter with your first husband? Or had he just broken the taboo of telling Malka to go fuck herself? Don't you realize how much she's screwed you all up?'

'She said you'd say that.'

'Oh, God, she's good. She's frightening. Listen, I can't clear this up overnight. Remove thirty-four years of brilliant brainwashing from your system. Do you love me, Rocky? If you love me, we've got a chance.'

He took her to Hawaii for six weeks and left the kids with his mother in Wyoming. They swam and laughed and ran in the surf. Graham had never seen her so happy. He'd left instructions with the hotel to refuse all phone calls from the mainland. He felt badly at first about tearing up the letters from Forest Hills before Rochelle had a chance to see them but then to clear his conscience he asked the desk clerk to return all letters 'address unknown'.

It was during the sixth week that Rochelle received a cable:

AM DESPERATELY ILL. DOCTORS ARE LYING TO ME. PLEASE RETURN AT ONCE.

MOTHER

'She's faking,' said Graham.

'How can you say that?'

Graham knew he should have kept his mouth shut but he heard himself answer: 'With very little difficulty.'

Rochelle grabbed the first plane back to the mainland. Graham fumed for an extra day then thought of Wyoming. He was too late. Rocky had arrived ahead of him and grabbed the kids. Upon his return to New York, Bochner hit him with divorce papers.

That was two years ago. She was in California with the kids and rumored to be marrying a marine biologist. Whoopee!

Graham stared at the list of telephone messages on his desk. He didn't know who any of these people were. Why had Miss Cable underlined Calvin Bennett in thick red crayon?

'He sounded very important,' Miss Cable said over the intercom. 'At least his secretary did.'

'Get me Bochner on the phone.'

Bochner sufficiently impressed Graham with Calvin Bennett's credit rating. CEO of HydroLux, a powerful industrial complex that had successfully invaded the European market after fifteen successful years in America.

Graham was also impressed by the fact a car was being sent for him and the secretary wanted to know his favorite brands of whisky and cigars.

The limousine drove into an underground garage beneath the Hydro-Lux Building on Avenue of the Americas. The door was opened for Graham, who was escorted along a tunnel passageway. They approached the doors of an elevator and the chauffeur said proudly: 'This car doesn't stop anywhere else except Mr. Bennett's private office.' Graham was getting the full treatment. There was still enough of the Wyoming cowboy in him to be impressed.

The chauffeur rode the elevator 35 floors down to the basement after Graham stepped out. Whoever the hell's directing this picture is an old hand, Graham thought to himself. Lawyer enters opulent office of international industrialist via a private elevator. Industrialist is deliberately not there to receive him thus giving the lawyer a few seconds to look the place over and be suitably impressed before—

'Mr. Graham?'

Graham immediately went on the defensive. Someone was in the room with as good a voice as his.

'I'm Calvin Bennett. Please sit down.'

Sitting down in that chair made Graham realize that he had never really sat before. Not like this. What comfort! What the hell was this chair made of? God's breath? This guy Bennett's very clever. Psyching me out with the chair. I better look uncomfortable.

'Something wrong with the chair?'

'No! YES! That is . . . Give me an old straight back wicker any day.' Oh, shit. I'm making an idiot out of myself with this guy. If only his voice wasn't so good. 'Guess I can get used to it.'

'I'll gladly get you another one.'

'No, no, no, no. Everything's fine.'

Graham stared hard at Calvin Bennett, who sat behind an enormous desk collecting his thoughts and rubbing his long, powerful fingers together. Three piece suit, wire glasses, fantastic poker face. Thank God the guy wasn't a district attorney.

Bennett got up from behind his desk and walked around its circumference to face Graham. The lawyer wasn't nuts about Bennett staring down at him. Bennett reached behind himself and produced a framed photograph.

'This is my son, Thomas Jefferson Bennett.'

Graham stared at the photograph of a young man in graduating robes. Black hair. Handsome face. Twenty-three or twenty-four.

Mr. Bennett reached behind himself again and returned with Photostatted documents.

'These are my son's academic scores at prep school and Yale. Also statements from various professors, civic leaders, clergymen, and other people with whom my son has come into contact through the years.'

Christ, this guy is good, Graham thought to himself. Even more frustrated than I am. He's probably been waiting all his life to play this scene. And for what? His son is probably some rich college punk, who had a little too much to drink. Went joyriding, bumped somebody off on the highway and fled from the scene of the accident. Let one of Bochner's boys handle this. Strictly Little League.

'My son is presently in Viet Nam.'

Whoops! I've sorely underestimated Calvin Bennett. This guy doesn't fool around. He's psyched me out with the chair, the picture, and the marks. Better not try and second guess him.

'Very proud of my son. Didn't try dodging the draft claiming bone spurs or some other chicken shit excuse.'

'I understand.' I don't understand a fucking thing. What is this case about?

Bennett produced another document and stared at it. He didn't share it with Graham.

'You're good, Graham. Some people say you're better than Belli or Foreman. "The Murder Man." Isn't that what they call you? Served in the army during Korea. Still in the reserves. Very convenient. They may make it difficult for us and say we can't have a civilian lawyer. That's okay. I can have you called up on 24 hours' notice. No need to discuss a fee. I'll present you with a blank check. Fill it in with whatever sum you want.'

Graham experienced a strange tingling sensation. Nothing in his experience to compare it with. Just the feeling this might be. . ..

'What is the charge?'

'Murder, of course,' replied Bennett rather testily. 'Doesn't your presence make that obvious?'

'Who is your son supposed to have murdered?'

Bennett passed him the document in his hand.

'You'll leave for Saigon as soon as possible. All expenses will be covered. My chauffeur is waiting for you in the tunnel.'

Saigon? Graham rode down in the elevator staring at seven names typed in alphabetical order:

Dixon, Millard Fillmore
Haynes, Arthur Lee
Kaplan, Robert
Keller, Dalton C.
Mackenzie, Bruce Arthur
Mendlsohn, Kenneth Paul
Rolingo, Ralph

# THE THREE RING CIRCUS

How long had Maxwell been standing in the rain? Seemed forever. The rain didn't bother him. He couldn't think of a single writer who'd died in the rain. He stood on the other side of the airport fence cutting an eccentric figure with the collar of his pajama tops sticking up from his raincoat, his drowned, king-sized cigarette bogarting down from his lips. One of John Milton's 'also-serves' standing and waiting for a plane that might never arrive.

'I'm waiting for a lady.'

The line had been running through Maxwell's head for days. Someone should publish a little, red, vest-pocket, book called 'Quotations from Humphrey Bogart'. Guaranteed best-seller. Good tight phrases to get a love-sick cynic through any problem. Particularly against assorted exotic backdrops in Africa or Asia. 'Of all the gin joints in all the towns in all the world she had to walk into mine.' Ain't it the truth! Love. Hopelessly, boyishly, desperately in love with a whore. To thine own self be true, Davie-boy. The lady *is* a tramp. But where the hell is she?

Whether Maxwell was really in love with Cashbox or not was of little importance. Something was needed to occupy his mind. He was finished as a writer. A laughingstock (or assumed he was). Couldn't even prove Milton Markson *existed*. Someone had done a bloody good job. They'd gotten to the Pentagon, the AMA, and the Bell Telephone Company seemingly overnight. God only knew where Estelle Markson was. Maxwell had sent cables to the Daughters of the American Revolution, the Parent Teachers Association of America, the Bnai Brith, Hadassah, and the North American Mah Jong League (that was Edelman's suggestion). Estelle might have been a patriot, but she certainly hadn't been a joiner.

The situation was farcical: everyone had known Dr. Markson, but it was impossible to legally document his existence.

There was no file on him at company headquarters. Claypoole fired forth fifteen epithets for all occasions then blatantly lied saying he'd never *heard* of Dr. Markson let alone set eyes on him. Harvey, wonderful Harvey, who had interviewed and run pictures of the lowest Vietnamese latrine cleaner didn't have a passing mention of Markson anywhere in the newspaper files.

Good-natured shouts of 'Found Dr. Markson yet?' greeted the correspondent wherever he walked. Maxwell began to wonder if the medical man had ever existed. Oh, no, he couldn't have made Milton up. Not with his theories on basketball, muscles and sex. Truth and illusion. Nothing is but isn't. What about the quarantine and the Wichita Ball Club? Had everyone forgotten about them?

Oh, Cashbox, where are you? Perhaps he'd missed her departing the plane. Didn't seem likely but it couldn't hurt to inquire. Maxwell stopped a tall, pock-marked captain who had stepped off the aircraft long after the others.

'Excuse me, Captain.'

The captain flashed an inquisitive pair of blue eyes and with a voice that had started from somewhere around his ankles countered with a striking, monosyllabic: 'Yes?'

'Did you notice a rather beautiful, young Asian girl on your flight?'

'Afraid not.'

'Thank you.'

The captain was heading towards the street when Maxwell realized who he was and chased after him.

'Captain! Captain! Mr. Graham!'

Graham turned around. He wasn't used to his new rank and was rather grateful to this Englishman for identifying him.

'Do we know each other?' Graham asked.

'You *are* Frank Graham?'

Graham stared at the disheveled man standing in front of him in a raincoat with pajama tops blooming forth at the neck. It couldn't be. Yes, of course. It was David Maxwell.

'David Maxwell?'

'Correct.'

'Hadn't expected anyone to meet me. I was told the press didn't know.'

'Know what?'

Graham paused. Bennett hadn't been bullshitting. If David Maxwell didn't know, no one knew.

At the same time Graham thought of his long-standing admiration for Maxwell and felt sorry for him about the Markson business. The story would have to come out some time soon. Why not give the Englishman the scoop?

'I'm here to handle a case,' Graham explained in his best semi-documentary, tough guy tones.

Maxwell's natural instincts started reacting.

'Murder?'

'That's my specialty.'

The correspondent grabbed the Murder Man's arm.

'Markson! They killed Markson! Right?'

'Not that I know of.'

It was a vain hope at best. David would have hated to see Milton with a knife in his back but it would have proved the poor sod's existence. Now there was nothing for Maxwell to do. He even made a token visit to Father Doolan, but the two-fisted god-man merely succeeded in drinking the correspondent under the table. Goddam whisky priest. Ought to be disrobed or banished or whatever one does to members of the clergy. Perhaps someone had killed Father Doolan, as well. No way. The steely-haired padre carried a Beretta with him everywhere. No. Then who got killed?

'My client is Thomas Jefferson Bennett. B Company.'

'That all you know about him?' Maxwell asked after a quick think.

'Oh, no. I know how quickly he can do the hundred yard dash. What his marks were in algebra in 1964-7. What clubs he served on at Yale. All the basics.'

It was a strange tingling sensation that David Maxwell was experiencing. There was nothing comparable in his personal history. Just the feeling that this might be *the* story. One question would confirm it.

'Do you know what platoon he's in?'

'Nope. Only that he's in B Company.'

Much as he regretted it, Maxwell had to stop the heavenly choir that was singing in his head. There was work to be done. Very quickly.

'Who is your client supposed to have murdered?'

Graham paused a second then opened his attaché case and handed the typed list to Maxwell.

'Mr. Graham, we can't talk here,' Maxwell said with considerable tension in his voice.

'What are—?'

'Shh. Trust me. We've got to get the hell out of this airport.'

'But what about your Asian friend?'

'Fuck her.'

Maxwell didn't say a word the entire ride to his apartment. Once inside he turned the radio up full blast then started to piece the mystery together.

'Who's in the Quonset hut?' Graham asked Maxwell.

'The surviving members of the platoon. And maybe Dr. Markson.'

'You mean there *is* a Dr. Markson?'

'Not you, too?'

'All I know is what I read in the papers,' apologized Graham.

'It was Dr. Markson who convinced me something wasn't kosher. Don't you find it strange the chief medical officer wouldn't know anything about the quarantine of an entire goddam platoon?'

'What about the quarantine?'

'There wasn't any bloody quarantine. Bennett bumped off those seven kids—'

'Excuse me,' interrupted Graham in his best direct from Mount Sinai voice. 'He is only *accused* of—'

'We're not in court. All right? I'm not fighting you. Simply shining some light on a potentially classic news story. *Someone* bumped off those seven kids in the jungle. They're blaming Bennett. They're terrified the story will leak out. With the Calley trial and the Green Berets, all they need is a mass murder of American soldiers *by* an American soldier. They erected the Quonset hut in a hurry and concocted the quarantine story to stall for time.'

'That is the ugliest—'

'It's what happened, mate!'

Maxwell got up and poured two stiff shots. He turned down the volume on the radio to ease the excitement and increasing tension in his system.

'Where is Bennett?' Maxwell asked Graham handing him the tumbler of scotch.

'Don't know. I know very little about this case. When you are virtually involved by an act of congress . . ..' Graham designated his uniform.

'Meant to ask you about that,' said Maxwell.

'Around two days ago - a little after midnight - my apartment house was the scene of a minor assault force who swore me back into the service, then dragged me into the gents at JFK two minutes before take-off and poured me into this uniform. . . Seems a civilian lawyer can't handle this case. They got around that by my being in the reserves.'

'Why would the army let you be recalled?' asked the correspondent. 'You're the defense counsel.'

'Money and the military go hand in hand,' shrugged Graham. 'Calvin Bennett is HydroLux. That can move mountains in Washington.'

'Why doesn't he just settle the whole thing there?'

'Not good for business. Bennett can pull strings for *me* but not his kid. It's one helluva case.'

'One helluva *monumental* case, Mr. Graham,' corrected Maxwell. 'And the gods have been kind enough to make us an important part of it.'

Maxwell stared deeply into Graham's eyes. The Murder Man returned his stare. Not a word was spoken but at that moment they became one. Their need was mutual. More than they'd ever needed anyone else in their respective lives. Fortunately, the need was matched by their mutual respect for each other's craft.

It was a rare and beautiful moment in their lives. For once Maxwell thought of Keats as something other than a pendant for depression. He finally appreciated and understood the silence upon the peak in Darien.


Fitzroy Claypoole had no regrets about being a career soldier. The army had done well by him and vice versa. As he had memorably declared at the 1963 Memorial Day Service: 'A soldier should not only wear his knapsack but *be* his knapsack.' That gave the men something to think about.

Remington had suggested Claypoole publish an anthology of *all* his epithets through the years. The Colonel had liked the idea at first then thought better of it. Remington was too damn pushy. Colonel Claypoole was six-feet-two-inches tall and Remington was half an inch taller. But Remington was skinny as a rake and had thinning hair. And he did not have Claypoole's nose.

The Colonel had three great passions: epithets, the Montana Cowboys, and his nose. It was a good nose. Big. No problems with asthma. Fitzroy had seen too many of his boyhood chums suffer from that affliction. His mother assured him it was only the size of his nose that had spared him from that torment. His mother's words had carried him proudly and inspiringly through life (despite the fact all the girls in high school called him 'Cyrano'). It was probably his nose that had kept him from marrying. He simply couldn't find a woman with a nose to match his. (This had nothing to do with pride but a care for genetics. No child of his would suffer from asthma. If it did happen, it certainly wouldn't be the parents' fault.)

Asthma was the furthest thought from his mind that day. Fitzroy Claypoole was feeling his oats. The situation was well in control. A lesser man might have panicked. But Fitzroy was a true son of Maryland. His boyhood chum, the Vice President, had called to congratulate him personally on the quarantine strategy. Claypoole had been in touch with the Veep a great deal since the election and it was rumored that Fitzroy himself had tailored the classic 'effete corps of impudent snobs'. No, it had all been routine. Granted there was a helluva lot of overtime. Look what he'd achieved virtually overnight. Erected a Quonset hut. Set up barbed wire. Started the quarantine rumor. All to give 'the big boys' the necessary time to plan their strategy.

If that hadn't been enough, there was the Markson business. He'd end up a five-star general the way he'd handled that crisis. Shut that goddam Englishman up, too. Claypoole only hoped no one wanted Markson back too soon.

Claypoole could not have been more loyal to Whitman's ship of state if he had tried. A closed-door court martial would take care of the whole unfortunate business neatly and efficiently. The boy would probably be discharged and confined to a mental institution. No one would ever know. Not a breath of scandal. No press hysteria. Heaven only knows the country had seen enough of that. Let them forge on and do their jobs. 'The work of a hoe is not helped by a ho.' Claypoole dashed to write that down before he forgot it.

Remington appeared in the doorway. The communications officer did not look well. Claypoole simply assumed that the skeletal, younger man had not fully recovered from his faint a fortnight before.

'What is it, Remington?'

'Don't know how to say this, sir.'

'Which is why I'm a colonel and you're a captain.'

'Remember when Mr. Maxwell made that statement at the press briefing?'

'And you fainted? I remember, Burnie. And I forgave you. Even though you needlessly "blew your cool", as the younger members of this company put it. Maxwell didn't know anything then and he knows nothing now. No reason he should. He's English. We beat them at Valley Forge, Yorktown, and New Orleans.'

'I agree he was bluffing then.' said Remington, then let the rest of his sentence hang.

'You *are* trying to tell me something. Well?'

The communications officer discovered he couldn't move his jaw.

'Remington, don't pull that frozen jaw routine with me. I have been patient with your rocking, soiling your trousers, and fainting. But this is too much, boy. Move that jaw and tell me what you've done.'

Remington resented the Colonel assuming it was something *he* had done. When he stopped to analyze it, it *was* his fault. He'd followed regulations informing Bennett's next of kin of the charges. How was he to know the boy's father was *Calvin* Bennett, who, in turn, would retain Frank Graham to defend his son?

The communications officer suddenly bolted from his commanding officer's office.

'Remington, get back here or I'll have you shot!!'

The communications officer returned a few seconds later. He'd merely dashed to his office to fetch the airmail editions of the newspapers that arrived on the afternoon plane. He placed them emotionally on the Colonel's desk.

'Sorry, sir,' said Remington, his jaw working again.

The headlines were all the same. David Maxwell had come up with the scoop of all time and broken the story on network television the night before. *Insight* would be hitting the streets the next day with a detailed special issue and an exclusive interview with Frank Graham.

The various papers not only described it as *the* scoop of the century but *the* scandal as well.

The accusations were horrifying. Responsibility might well lead up to the highest link in the chain of command. The repercussions would be felt all the way down. Never in the course of human endeavor had so many been up shit's creek with so few paddles.

'What is it, Colonel?'

'Nothing.'

'Are you sure, sir? You're shaking.'

Fitzroy Claypoole *was* shaking. The newspapers had affected him in a way he had never dreamed of. He was experiencing a physical phenomenon that had never happened to him before: His nose was plugged.

Maxwell shook his head in amazement as he walked around the base. As a working journalist for fifteen years, he'd covered earthquakes, beauty contests, minor revolutions, and student demonstrations. But he'd never seen so many foreign press flowing into Saigon.

'They may have to close the country this year,' Maxwell said to Graham as they sat in the correspondent's living room.

'I have the funniest feeling it's the United States of America on trial,' answered Graham.

'It is, mate. Believe me. Everybody loves a lynching. They're hoping you'll crucify the republic.'

'I'm trying to save a boy's life.'

'Lucky if that even comes into it.'

'Maybe I shouldn't have taken the case,' suggested Graham. 'No?'

'No,' said Maxwell. 'I just don't envy you. Fighting the greatest power in the world. Truly heroic. In the true classical sense. They're going to fire every big gun at you they can. No, I don't envy you. But I admire you.'

The telephone rang and Maxwell sprang for it. He listened intently and said very little. Then he muttered. 'Good boy, Harvey,' and hung up. 'My leg-man. Went for a walk and discovered something very interesting. The Quonset hut is gone.'

'What!?'

'Hard to believe, isn't it? Big thing like that. Apparently, there's a huge grass stain where the sun never shone for three weeks.'

'Hmmm. Technically, you realize, the Quonset hut isn't even necessary to the case.' said Graham.

'It's *extremely* necessary to the story *behind* the case,' replied Maxwell.

'Like Dr. Markson?'

'Like Dr. Markson.'

Graham began to have a vision of the future. The collaboration with Maxwell he'd once imagined was quickly becoming a reality.

A slight touch of humility came into Graham's voice as he suggested to Maxwell the court might find some of these details irrelevant to the actual charge.

'But this is a military trial,' countered Maxwell, 'They're going to want to know *all* the facts. Don't worry, Frank, we're on the same side.'

If there was a war going on it was being fought prominently in the bar of the press club. Or in the press club proper which was one big bar. There simply weren't enough bartenders to handle all the action and there wasn't enough fresh daily news to satisfy the demands of the correspondents' editors back at their respective home bases. Bribes and outrageous lies soon became the order of the day. Press liaison was almost non-existent since the base commander had gone into the hospital.

Claypoole had foolishly (or brilliantly) left Remington in charge of all press releases and official statements. All the poor Philadelphian could do was rock back and forth mumbling quotations from Ayn Rand. This satisfied some of the more conservative papers but was getting him nowhere with the eastern bloc or Barry Lomax.

Lomax was a veteran of twenty years all over the world. The Australian-born journalist knew the courtesies due a reporter. How many free drinks and sandwiches were coming to him and how high he could pad his expense account. He also knew when a press officer was fumbling to cover or when he simply didn't know. This idiot Remington didn't know a dingo from a donut.

But who did? And know what? It was like a three-ring circus. Never knew where to direct your attention. One day the Quonset hut was there, then—bingo! Vanished. Lomax finally found out the surviving members of the platoon had been broken up and reassigned to different companies. Addresses unknown. Where was Bennett? Would there be a press conference? Would Graham let anyone talk to him? More importantly, would Maxwell let anyone talk to Graham? Whole thing was being handled like a William Morris package. There was no one to complain to. No code of ethics to hold up. Besides, it *was* Maxwell. And Maxwell was the journalist's journalist.

Remington now had a new problem. Colonel Claypoole had telephoned from the hospital ordering him to send the bodies back to America. Remington didn't know where the bodies were.

He reached for the telephone and rang PFC Harvey Edelman.

'Edelman! Captain Remington here.'

'Yes, sir.'

Remington thought twice before answering and hung up the phone. Edelman immediately dialed Maxwell. Within minutes Maxwell was in Remington's office making the communications officer's life miserable.

'What do you want here?' asked Remington, cowering in a corner of the office like some vampire's prey.

'Captain, this is your office. Please, sit down,' smiled Maxwell.

Remington edged towards his desk then bounded into his chair as if there was a possibility it might not be there a second later.

'I gather something's wrong,' said the correspondent in his best bedside manner.

'You can't help me,' blurted out Remington.

'One never knows till one tries.'

Something very convincing and very soothing resided in Maxwell's manner. Remington melted and became almost child-like. He couldn't understand why he'd been frightened of the Englishman. Maxwell was a nice man.

'If I help you find the bodies, will you tell me where Dr. Markson is?'

'I don't know', wailed Remington. 'I woke up one morning and he was gone . . . Does that mean you won't help me with the bodies?'

'Of course not, Burnett. Come on.'

'Where are we going?'

'To the morgue. Graves Registration.'

Maxwell rang Harvey Edelman first and told the private to meet them with his Minolta camera.

Edelman had been rather queasy at first about identifying the bodies of his fellow soldiers. After the first few snapshots he simply pretended they were asleep. There *was* a rather peaceful look about their faces in the cold storage room. Death had come quickly and without pain.

Maxwell paused a second before the body of Millard Fillmore Dixon then snapped his picture with the Minolta.

'There are your bodies, Captain,' he said finally.

'Thank you.' Remington answered sincerely. 'If there's ever anything I can do for you, Mr. Maxwell—'

'Get these boys home. They've been waiting a long time.'

Cleet Fowler was worried about The Boss. He hadn't visited him in the hospital for fear of embarrassing him. Now that The Boss was home

Fowler felt he should pay his respects and see if he wanted any heads busted.

Ever since Colonel Claypoole expressed a desire to manage the Montana Cowboys when they left the service, Fowler affectionately referred to his commanding officer as The Boss. The Colonel referred to Fowler with equal fondness as Cleet-boy.

For the first seventeen years of his life, Cleet Fowler believed his mother had been a grizzly bear. He'd never known his real mother and whenever he had asked his Pa about her the elder Fowler said his Ma 'had been a big old grizzly bear I made love to up in the mountains'. There was no reason to disbelieve it. Fowler looked like a grizzly bear. Which isn't the best shape to be for a baseball pitcher. But that didn't stop Sergeant Fowler from throwing the deadliest pitches in South-East Asia.

Fowler found out his mother wasn't a grizzly bear when he went for his army physical. He almost busted the examining doctor's head open for lying to him about his Ma. After they pulled Fowler off the doctor they explained it was impossible for him to have been sired by a bear. They showed him charts. They explained the facts of life. They discovered that Cleet Fowler was a moron. But he was a patriotic moron, who was more than willing to die and kill for his country. His intelligence tests were conveniently misplaced and he was welcomed with open arms into the service. Eight years later Fowler still had a home in the army and a new father in Fitzroy Claypoole.

The Sergeant was shown upstairs to the Colonel's bedroom where Claypoole lay in bed reading the *Wall Street Journal* wearing a handsome, velvet dressing gown.

'Hello, Cleet-boy.'

'Hello, boss.'

The Colonel rubbed the top of the Fowler's head affectionately and the Sergeant presented him with a package of Oreo cookies he'd purchased that morning on the black market.

'Mighty good of you, boy,' said Claypoole. The Colonel discovered whenever he was with Fowler he assumed a rather home-spun style of frontier speech which was lately creeping into his conversation with his officers.

'Reckoned I ought to have brought somethin' . . . boss.' Fowler had wanted to say 'Pa' but knew it was against regulations. Since his own Pa had died four years before he thought of The Boss as his Pa.

'They keepin' you busy, boy?' the Colonel asked.

'Much as they can.'

The two sat and nodded smilingly at each other. The scene was ridiculous. The bumpkin, grizzly-bear Sergeant sitting on the edge of the bed with the silver-temple Colonel decked out in a Noel Coward dressing gown nibbling on Oreo cookies.

'How's your nose?' Fowler asked.

'Fine, boy, fine. I can smell the flowers again. . .. And the asthma?'

Claypoole was haunted day and night by the fear that Fowler might develop asthma. He couldn't bear to think of this lovable grizzly bear wheezing through life, or worst, on the pitcher's mound. There was nothing wrong with Fowler's breathing. The only thing Fowler suffered from was crabs.

'Been to see a doctor about them?' asked Claypoole.

'You know I have, Boss. Dr. Markson was treating me—'

'Shh. Shh.' Claypoole put a hand to Fowler's mouth. 'You're not supposed to mention his name anymore.'

'Sorry.'

'That's all right.' Claypoole continued munching on an Oreo then asked his visitor: 'Remember where you put him yet?'

Fowler thought long and hard then answered: 'No. Are you mad at me?'

'No, Cleet-boy. Don't you fret none. Everything's going to be all right.'

'What about this here court martial? And that goddam English feller?'

'There may not be a court martial. Maybe just a hearing.' Fowler's brow wrinkled. He was confused. 'Don't you go worrying your head about it. I had Mr. Santiago on the phone again from Washington. He's sending a cracker-jack prosecutor out here to handle everything. He might even come himself.'

'Then we can play ball again, boss?'

'No reason in the world why we can't.'

Fowler got up from the bed and saluted his commanding officer.

'Thanks, Pa.' The grizzly bear turned and marched down the stairs.

Claypoole took a deep, long, happy breath. Nothing wrong with his nose now. He felt good. Damn good. What had Fowler called him? 'Pa'. Claypoole liked the sound of it. Nice word. Pa.

# THE PRISONER

Graham tried twice to see Tommy Bennett but was informed by Dr. Renfrew that the boy was still under sedation. The lawyer began to worry his client might 'accidentally' stay under sedation forever. But three days after Graham's arrival the boy was released from hospital and transferred to the maximum-security section of the stockade.

During those three days, the lawyer had worked methodically gleaning information about the Wichita Platoon. He knew everything about them before they went into the jungle and after they came out. What had happened *in* the jungle was as much a mystery as ever. 'When I walked into the jungle, I was seventeen. When I walked out I was twenty-one. And, by God, I was rich!' That didn't work. Tommy Bennett had walked in 24 and walked out 24 - just as rich upon entering as leaving.

'Tommy Bennett couldn't have done it,' a voice said to Graham on the third day as he stared at the information he had accumulated.

Graham looked up at the private staring over his shoulder. It was that Edelman kid, who ran errands for Maxwell. There was something about the kid Graham didn't like.

'You don't like me,' said Edelman.

'Did I say that?' asked an irritated Graham. 'I don't even know your name . . . Edelman, isn't it?'

Harvey hadn't liked the way the lawyer had groped for and pronounced 'Edelman'. It reminded him of the way his first-year high-school teacher had called him up to the front of the class to present his note for being absent from school on the Jewish New Year. 'Hope this won't occur again, Edelman,' said the teacher. Poor Harvey found himself apologizing to the man for the fact he would be away again the following week, and the third and the fourth. Harvey had been the only Jew in his St. Louis classroom.

'No need to be anti-Semitic about it,' Edelman said.

'Who's anti-Semitic?'

'Please, let's not prolong this,' replied hit-and-run Edelman.

'No, no. Let's have this out here and now. What did I say that you regard as anti-Semitic? I didn't even know you were Jewish. Still don't. Are you?'

'Whether I'm Jewish or not has nothing to do with an anti-Semitic remark.'

'Beauty in the eye of the beholder?' asked Graham. 'How do you know I'm not Jewish?'

'Who said Jewish? I said Semitic. How do you know I'm not an Arab?'

'Are you an Arab?' asked Graham.

'No. Are you Jewish?'

'Of course not.'

'Aha!'

'What do you mean 'aha'?'

'You've betrayed yourself!'

'Edelman, you're insane!' roared Graham. 'I'm not anti-Semitic. My wife was Jewish.'

'Was?' asked Edelman. 'Is she dead?'

'No. We're divorced.'

'Aha!'

Graham paused and stared at Edelman. The kid had potential. Fantastic sense of assault. Good courtroom style. Unfortunately, he had the same whining, nasal, sing-song voice Bochner was afflicted with. But that wasn't what had bothered Graham. Nor was it a question of anti-Semitism. He suddenly realized what it was about Edelman that bothered him. The kid wore glasses.

'How did you get in the army with those glasses?'

'I—I volunteered,' stammered Edelman, who had not seen this question coming out of right field.

'What for?' asked an amazed Graham.

'I wanted to see the war. Thought it would help me grow up.'

Graham paused for a moment then asked: 'What's your first name?'

'Harvey.'

'You're going to be all right, Harvey.'

The lawyer started to walk away then stopped and turned around to the soldier.

'Why couldn't he have done it?'

'They were the best friends Tommy had on earth.'

Graham said nothing in reply and resumed walking towards the stockade.

Edelman felt much better. The day was going well for him now. Graham liked him. Or so it seemed. At least he wasn't anti-Semitic. Maybe that's what Mr. Maxwell had been talking about. Maybe it was just Harvey's hang-up. It was nice to know he could talk to Graham in the future. That and the Chy Ming story were making for a very nice day in the life of PFC Harvey Edelman.

The Chy Ming story had made a convenient break in the monotonous uncertainty of Tommy Bennett's imprisonment. There really wasn't anything new to say about Bennett's case. Nothing that hadn't been printed over and over again to the point of redundancy. Edelman was a sworn enemy of redundancy (even before Colonel Claypoole made it an in thing).

Chy Ming was fresh news and no one else had bothered to cover it except Harvey.

Far off in the mountains many centuries before there lived a man named Chy Ming. He was a guerilla bandit, an oriental Robin Hood, a myth whose true history had long been forgotten. Every village had a different story about Chy Ming. The bandit was the essence of hope, a spirit who lived in the mountains and was fabled to return to his people's aid when they most needed him. His mountain kingdom was one of peace and pleasure. Many of the village elders spoke of going to live with Chy Ming when their days were numbered.

When a supply truck had been attacked on its way through the mountains the night before everyone assumed it was either the black market or the Cong. But the driver had been told to tell everyone it was the work of Chy Ming, who was in the mountains waiting for others to join him.

The story had appealed to Harvey's basic sense of romance. He gave it page one coverage pushing news of the Bennett trial on to the second page.

The last person he expected to react to it was David Maxwell but a few minutes later the correspondent had buttonholed him on the parade ground.

'Harvey, what are you doing?' Maxwell asked, holding out a copy of the base paper in front of him.

'I don't understand.'

'What is this story, Edelman? Haven't you learned anything from me? Thought you wanted to be a journalist.'

'I do.'

'This is bloody *True Magazine*. You've got a first-degree murder on your hands. Don't abandon it because there's a lull. You should be searching all the time. Like I am. What is this rot about some bandit in the mountains?'

'Thought it was a good story,' said Edelman, trying to defend his journalistic judgement.

'It's pulp fiction. The Viet Cong's knocking over supplies left and right. So's the black market. We all know that, lad. This isn't the Spanish Civil War, Harvey. There aren't any heroes. My advice to you, kid, is drop this Chy Ming business before it becomes a joke.'

Edelman felt he was about to cry. His whole day was ruined. He had fallen out of grace with his idol. Maybe Maxwell was right. Maybe? Who was he kidding? This was David Maxwell. There were no maybe's involved. Edelman should be damn grateful the man was taking time to bother criticizing him.

'Sorry, Mr. Maxwell.'

'It's all right, kid. Bloody awful morning. But watch it in future. Have you seen Frank Graham?'

'He was going towards the stockade.'

'Thanks.'

Maxwell saw Remington drive by in a jeep and flagged him down.

Captain Remington had failed his driver's license test repeatedly when he'd been a civilian, so he took advantage of his rank and was continually commandeering jeeps much to the despair of the motor pool. He dearly loved driving. Despite the fact he didn't know what the hell he was doing, he was never happier than when he was behind the wheel of some motor vehicle. Burnt-out clutches. Demolished gear boxes. Dented fenders. Cracked headlamps. They were someone else's worry. And the bills never came to him.

'Do you get some kind of kick out of this?' Maxwell asked as he swallowed his intestines for the third time and noticed that the stockade was somewhere in the vague vicinity of Remington's demonic meanderings.

'The only relaxation I get,' Remington answered gaily, standing up so his head was over the windscreen. He was holding the top of the steering wheel with his left hand and waving frantically with his right for innocent soldiers to get out of the way.

'Remember that favor you owe me?' Maxwell shouted as they careered round the flagpole in the center of the parade ground.

'Me and the elephant.'

'Yeah. Well, stop the jeep, Dumbo.'

The captain glided the machine to a halt with the sheer control of a seasoned air-line pilot.

'Not a bad landing.' Remington said proudly.

'How the hell did you get a license?' gasped the correspondent.

'I haven't got one.'

'Want to fly? Join the bloody Air Force,' said Maxwell, making sure his feet were firmly on the ground and that no part of his body was touching the jeep.

'Something wrong with my driving?'

'Have I offended you? So sorry.'

'Your conversation has taken on a needlessly sarcastic tone. This coupled with ingratitude—'

'Ingratitude!?'

'This is a military vehicle designed for—'

'You could have fooled me. I thought it was a ride at a bloody fun fair!!'

'Where I come from, Mr. Maxwell—'

'Sounds like the prelude for a challenge to a duel.'

Remington was fuming. He hadn't intended going that far. A duel! Was a lack of good manners enough reason for a duel? It had been in the last century. But it was this century and people didn't duel. Or did they? One certainly didn't read about it in the newspapers. But look who was controlling the newspapers. The Vice President had personally spoken to Colonel Claypoole enough about that subject and the Colonel told Remington everything the Vice President told him. Aha! It all made sense. People who fought duels all worked for newspapers. That's why one never read about them. It was all hushed up. Countless duels were probably being fought in composing rooms all over America. Blood intermingled with type. That's what it meant to have printer's ink in one's veins. And this man Maxwell was a deadly practitioner. The very fact the Englishman was alive made him living proof. Well, he wouldn't find Burnett C. Remington another hotheaded, gullible victim.

'May I ask where you're going, Mr. Maxwell?'

'No. Yes! I'm going to the stockade.'

'Do you have any business there?'

Maxwell drew in a deep breath and pointed to the jeep.

'That is a military vehicle. These are civilian feet.' The correspondent turned and walked towards the stockade.

Arriving at the stockade, Maxwell discovered Graham was nowhere in sight. The lawyer arrived a few minutes later vehemently cursing two maniacs who had almost run him down with a jeep a few minutes before.

'Did you get a letter today?' asked Maxwell.

'What kind of letter?'

'From Bennett?'

'No, but I had some vague communication from the legal department of Omnipress. Whatever the hell that is.'

'Frank, you've got to teach me how to imitate the ostrich.'

'What do you mean?' Although the lawyer wouldn't admit it, he'd been having a bit of difficulty the last three days keeping up with some of the Englishman's cryptic allusions.

'Omnipress is a multi-billion-dollar conglomerate. They own HydroLux—'

'Doesn't Calvin Bennett—?'

Maxwell shook his head: 'He's loaded but he ain't it. Found that out in my letter this morning. Special delivery from Frawley. *Insight* is published by Frawley but is part of the Omnipress conglomerate.'

'We're both working for the same people,' said Graham, over-simplifying the situation.

'What did your letter say, Frank?'

'More of a memo than a letter. "The interests of Omnipress and HydroLux are one and the same."'

'Which is a warning not to step on anyone's toes,' added Maxwell. 'Going to ride this one out?'

'How do you mean?'

'If they try to pull you off the case, will you stay with it?'

'Why would—?'

'Will you?'

'Yes.'

'All I wanted to know. Let's go talk to the kid.'

Graham was getting pissed off at Maxwell. All this cryptic mumbo-jumbo about conglomerates and stepping on toes. Why didn't he just say what he meant? Collaborators are supposed to collaborate. Maxwell was running the whole show. But not once they got into court. Maybe that's why he was hogging the limelight now. Let him write all the words he wants. It was Graham's voice that was going to do all the talking in front of those TV cameras with the satellites beaming the trial into every country in the world. Preminger was bound to see it somewhere.

Tommy Bennett lay on the cot in his cell trying to sort out the mess of his life. Hard to concentrate. Too many dream-like elements. Voices coming in and out of existence. Footsteps. Rifle clips. Silent screams. There had been a patrol. Like any other patrol. Search and destroy. Don't drop anyone out of a helicopter. Don't take pictures. Don't commit atrocities. A few more months and homeward bound. Back to what? Anything but this. They split into three. Kip took six guys. Ramirez took five. The Sergeant took another five. Bennett, you stay here and guard the supplies. If we're not back in an hour . . . What? What, Sarge? What if you aren't back in an hour? Stupid Polack idiot. Why don't you finish the sentence? Waiting. Waiting, waiting, waiting.

Everything after that became vague. Like the wrong end of a telescope. He had woken up in the base hospital dripping in perspiration. His mind was racked with faceless dreams. Strange flying philgrims. Philgrims? What the hell were philgrims? Whatever they were, they were flying low and heading for Tommy. He ducked and fell out of the bed. The nurses sent for Dr. Renfrew, and he was strapped down.

The tumble had brought him down in more ways than one. Lying flat on his back, he took in the situation. Why wasn't he in the ward? Why weren't any other soldiers with him? Unless he was—He looked about. There was no nurse in the room. Unbuckling the belt across his chest, he lifted the sheet. He examined his body. No visible marks or scars. His feet hurt like hell. Probably from the boots and marching. But where was everyone else? Why was he being kept in isolation? Where was he?

Hearing footsteps coming down the corridor, he quickly fastened the belt across his chest. Two nurses entered followed by Dr. Renfrew. What day was it? They had gone into the jungle Friday morning. The boys had split up in the afternoon. Then the vagueness. The philgrims started flying then. Like Quakers on broomsticks. Wow! He was still tripping. Maybe the hospital was part of it. He was on some big medical trip. Hi! I'm on a big medical trip. Obstetrics, Denver. Gynecology, Seattle. Never shake hands. Better bring this ship in for a landing.

'Where are the other guys?' asked Tommy Bennett feebly.

Renfrew gestured for the nurses to leave the room.

'You've had a pretty bad time,' said Renfrew.

'Have I?' asked young Bennett. He was his father's son in many ways and far from awe-struck by medical men.

'What's wrong with me, doctor?'

'You need rest now.'

'Where are the other guys?'

'We'll have you up on your feet as soon as possible.'

'Why am I in a separate room?'

'Lie back and relax.'

'Am I a security risk?' asked Tommy mockingly. 'I want to get back to my platoon. We're supposed to be playing a ball game. I may have missed it. Have they played already? Who won?'

'Do I to have to call the guards?'

'Guards? What guards? What the hell's going on? Hey, doc. Come on. Let me in on it, will you? What am I doing in here?' His voice cracked on the last sentence and his body started to shake.

Dr. Renfrew rang for a nurse.

'Hypo.'

'What do I need a needle for?'

'Help you relax and get some sleep.'

'I'm relaxed enough now.' Tommy said as he watched Renfrew squirt some liquid out of the needle. 'I've been sleeping forever. Don't want to sleep anymore. Want to get up. Want to play ball. We have to win . . . .'

Imitate the action of the armadillo. Roll into a furry shape and protect yourself against the buffets along the way as you hurtle headlong down the tunnel. When he finally stopped rolling, Colonel Claypoole was standing in front of him surrounded by MPs. Captain Remington was in the room as well. And Fowler. What was Fowler doing there? The Colonel was holding up an official looking document and advising Tommy not to say anything until proper counsel had been secured for him. The document said Tommy had killed Kip, Rolingo, Keller, Fingers and Buzz. And Punjab and the Asp. Wow! Time to wake up. That was the scary part. He couldn't wake up. It wasn't a dream. It was really happening. His seven buddies were dead. And he was accused of. . . Please, God! Let it be a nightmare. Let me wake up. I'll be a good boy. Just let me wake up.

He fell further into sleep. Dreamless sleep. Somewhere between two stars. Total vacuum. He was content. A long peaceful sleep.

Bennett came to attention when the captain entered his cell.

'At ease. At ease. Cool it,' said Graham, not used to young men coming to attention and saluting when they saw him.

Tommy sat down on his bunk again and stared at the tall, pock-marked officer with the voice of God. Something very familiar about his face.

'My name's Frank Graham. I'm your lawyer.'

'Aren't you the Murder Man?'

'That's right.'

'Did my father hire you?' Tommy laughed. 'Wow! Too much. The last of the big spenders. For my twenty-first birthday, he wanted to hire the Stones and the Supremes to sing in shifts.'

'Glad you've got a sense of humor.'

'Have I?' asked Tommy.

Graham took out a cigarette and lit it. This was his smoking bit. Almost a ritual on the first encounter with the client. Usually followed by the jacket coming off and the tie loosened. He decided to wait a bit with the jacket and the tie.

'Smoke?' he asked, extending the pack to Tommy.

The boy stared at the cigarettes and said nothing. Graham was beginning to think him a bit simple then he remembered Tommy's academic scores. The boy was simply dazed.

'Yeah,' Tommy said a second later taking a cigarette from the pack.

'Where do you want to start?' Graham asked.

Bennett shrugged his shoulders. There wasn't that much he could tell the lawyer, but he began with the patrol and how the platoon split into three leaving him behind to guard the supplies.

'Then what happened?' asked Graham.

'I don't know . . . Next thing I remember was being in the hospital.'

Graham took off his jacket and loosened his tie.

'I'm not here to serve moral judgement on you, Tommy. Whether you killed those boys or not, my job is to save your life. I can't do that unless you help me. . . Certain holes must be filled in.'

'I'm all for that, Mr. Graham. There are three weeks missing from my life.'

The boy was calm, slightly angry, but not nervous. Tough, too. If he's a liar, he's a pro. That'll come out soon enough.

'How long were you in the Quonset hut before they moved you?' asked Graham.

'What Quonset hut?'

'Don't piss me around, Tommy.'

'Mr. Graham, will you answer me one question? Why was I in the hospital to begin with? I'll take my clothes off right here. There's not a mark on me. Seen my medical charts? What do they say?'

Graham smiled. Goddam fresh kid. He and Edelman should open an office together: Attack Incorporated. The charts were a good point. He'd have to check on them later.

'I assumed you'd know,' said Graham.

'That's an over-assumption,' Bennett said grimly. 'When's my trial?'

'Don't know. It's all being played by ear. Conflict of interests. But we better get some of our facts together, boy, or we're going to be in big trouble.'

Graham quickly recapped the whole story of the Quonset hut, its kubrickian appearance and recent disappearance. He also described the worldwide press coverage it had received and the furor that rocked Washington after Maxwell had broken the story.

'I have no recollection whatsoever of the Quonset hut, Mr. Graham. I swear to you.'

'It's possible they moved you straight into the hospital to keep an eye on you. Then the Quonset hut went up quickly and they stuck the rest of the guys in there as a cover.'

'The quarantine story?'

'Right. As far as the world was concerned the platoon was still alive. That gave them enough time to figure out some kind of strategy.'

'You keep saying "them" and "they", said Bennett. 'Who?'

Tommy had emphasized the last question with his hand. Graham noticed something he hadn't seen before and grabbed the boy's hand.

'That hurt?'

'What?'

Graham pointed to a large, fresh scar across the top of Bennett's right hand.

'How long have you had that?' asked the Murder Man.

'Never saw it before in my life.'

'Thought you checked yourself for scars.'

'I did,' answered Tommy, 'all over my body.' He emphasized the statement by running his hands down his torso. He stopped and laughed. 'Everywhere except my hands.'

'You didn't have that scar before you went into the jungle?'

'Positive.'

Graham leaned back on the cot and lit another cigarette. He thought about Wyoming. When he was a freshman at college everyone would kid him about being from the wide-open spaces and he resented it. But in recent years he came to think of Wyoming as a refuge, a place to go—most often mentally—when his worry quotient was rising. He was very much in Wyoming now. Thousands of miles from where he should have been.

'Think it's a clue?' asked Tommy.

'Just a second.' answered Graham.

Just because this case is a mess doesn't mean I have to get caught in the chaos. A little order. Little organization. A few steps back and about a mile up in the air. Much better. What have we got? Frank Graham sent for by wealthy robber baron to defend his son on murder charge. The charge is murder. In order to have a charge there must be an accusation. Who accused who? Somebody is holding back a helluva lot of evidence. This case isn't going anywhere until—

'I was shot.'

'What?'

'I was shot,' repeated Tommy.

'Who shot you?'

'Ramirez.'

'When?'

'Don't know. Can't remember.'

'Why would Ramirez want to shoot you?'

'I don't know,' said Thomas Jefferson Bennett. Then he asked bitterly: 'Why would I want to shoot *them?*'

# THE HOOKER AND THE GOD-MAN

Fitzroy Claypoole was back on his feet and 'full of beans' (to quote himself). The nose was 'in tiptop shape'. In fact, the world had never looked brighter. The Colonel felt a certain sense of omniscience. Possibly because he had put Sergeant Fowler and the Montana Cowboys on permanent guard duty at the stockade. No man could have a more devoted and trustworthy network of spies. It was the Colonel's intention not 'to let the prosecution be caught with their pants down' and, through Cleet Fowler and the boys, he would share every bit of information and strategy that passed between Graham and Bennett.

He was a little annoyed at this Ramirez business. Renfrew assured him Bennett wouldn't remember anything. Santiago wouldn't like this new wrinkle. But Santiago need never know. After all, no one spoke to Santiago except Claypoole. The Colonel would deal with the Ramirez business himself. Have to get some sort of chart smuggled into the hospital file. Not he personally. Good heavens, no! That was Remington's job. He leaned forward in his chair and buzzed the captain on the intercom. No answer.

'Where is that fool?' the Colonel muttered to himself as he strode down the hall towards the communications officer's office. If he was hiding behind the door again . . .

Captain Remington's office was empty. The Colonel checked his desk to see if the communications officer had been polite enough to leave a note explaining his absence. The only thing he found on the memo pad was: 'Speak to the Colonel regarding CIVILIAN FEET.' What the hell were civilian feet? The boy was cracking up. Understandable. His nose was far too small for his height.

Claypoole left Remington's office and collided with a captain he had never seen before.

'Ah! Colonel Claypoole. Just the man I wanted to see,' said Graham, flashing a big grin.

The Colonel stared at the lunatic in front of him. Was this man a fugitive from Bedlam Hospital? Had he no concept of order? What sort of way was this to greet a superior officer?

'Who the devil are you?' demanded Claypoole.

'Frank Graham.'

'*Captain* Graham,' corrected Claypoole. 'You're wearing a uniform. A symbol, sir. Ever wear a symbol before?'

'Yes, sir. 52-54.'

'Korea. See any action?'

'Not the kind you mean,' grinned Graham.

'Goddamit, man. We're not playing toy soldiers here. Come to attention.'

Graham immediately regretted taking the case. The uniform hadn't bothered him until to now. Everyone he'd encountered so far was either of lower rank or a civilian. He couldn't care less whether non-coms saluted him or not. But he hadn't counted on running into General Patton here. Oh, well. Humor the guy.

'Listen, Colonel—'

'No. You listen to *me*, Mr. Fancy Toy-Soldier-Lawyer-Visitor-Intruder.' The Colonel took a deep breath, impressed with the string he had just let loose. Without even thinking. He'd have to mark them down when he got back to the office. Yes, indeed. Quite an impressive string. He hurried back towards his office while the words were still fresh—

'Sir!'

Claypoole looked back and saw Graham still frozen at attention.

'At ease, Captain.'

'How about ''Stand easy''?'

'I don't like—'

'Please!'

'All right, what is it?' asked Claypoole, throwing the soldier-lawyer-visitor-intruder a meaningful let-that-be-a-lesson-to-you look.

'I'd like to speak to you about Private Bennett.'

'Private Bennett is none of your business.'

'I'm his lawyer,' retorted the Murder Man getting angry.

Colonel Claypoole decided he did not like Captain Graham at all. The man was a disgrace to his uniform. Wasn't even his uniform. The Colonel had been informed—much to his disgust—how Graham delayed a commercial airliner in New York to play soldier in the men's room. Oh, no! This smart-ass would get short shrift from Fitzroy Claypoole.

'Would you like to come into my office?' asked the Colonel with a smoother-than-smooth cordiality.

Graham smiled his thanks. Maybe things were looking up. It was simply a question of understanding the Colonel's point of view. The guy was a professional soldier who expected the usual courtesies that went with the job. No reason why he should give Graham special treatment. After all, he was just another uniform. Of lower rank.

The Colonel put his hand on the doorknob and noticed he still had Remington's memo in his hand. He gave the memo to Graham.

'What do you make of that?' he asked the lawyer.

'What are civilian feet?'

'That's why I'm a Colonel and you're a Captain,' Claypoole answered smugly. Inside himself, he was disappointed. He was hoping Graham might be able to explain the cryptic note.

'What *does* it mean, Colonel?

Claypoole was on the spot. Hadn't counted on Graham carrying on with the topic. Remington never would have. Remington didn't have balls enough to question his commanding officer. Still, Remington had written it, and that had taken balls enough. Obviously some sort of code. But for what? Possibly Remington had defected to Graham and the Englishman. Must speak to Cleet-boy about that later. Meanwhile, something must be said to throw Graham off the track. A red herring. The Colonel's eyes caught the headline of the base newspaper. Something about a bandit.

'Does the name Chy Ming mean anything to you?'

'No, sir.'

'You haven't the slightest idea what I'm up against, Captain Graham.' While he spoke, the Colonel scanned the rest of the article trying to glean as much information about Chy Ming as he could. Was Edelman out of his mind? Why was he publishing all this rubbish? The Colonel had a war to run. He didn't need his men distracted by plots straight out of Terry and the Pirates. He'd have words with Edelman later. Might as well string Graham along with it for now.

'Ahem, Graham. You haven't been given sufficient security clearance. I'm not at liberty to discuss Chy Ming with you. But I *can* tell you that there is a definite link between Chy Ming and civilian feet. Trust this conversation won't leave the room.' Claypoole counted on Graham discussing it immediately with Maxwell.

'You have nothing to worry about, sir.'

'Good. Anything else I can do for you?'

Graham was lost. Way back. The minute he saw 'civilian feet'. Then Chy Ming. That was the topper. Was Chy Ming a disease or the specialty at Lichee Gardens? That s.o.b. Claypoole played dirty, and he didn't have a bad voice, either. Think, Frank. What did you want to see him about? Get back on your feet. They haven't counted ten yet.

'I'd like to see Tommy Bennett's medical records, sir.'

'This isn't the hospital', smiled the Colonel, lighting a cigarette and fitting it into the holder.

'You mean I can get his file from the hospital?'

'I mean his file is at the hospital, but you can't get it.'

'Why not?'

'Dr. Renfrew has quite enough to do without you disrupting his procedure and monopolizing his staff to look at a chart that would mean nothing to a layman.'

'Suppose I get a technical witness to interpret it for me?'

'Like whom?'

'Like Dr. Markson.'

The Colonel didn't blink.

The Murder Man was frustrated. That trick had always worked before. Claypoole was a sharp customer.

'We've exhausted the conversation, Captain.'

'I don't think so,' said the lawyer assuming his best documentary, two-fisted racket-buster voice. 'Let's take the gloves off, Colonel. You're covering up for somebody and when I find out—for all your shiny medals—you won't be able to get a job as a doorman.'

God, that sounded good! Straight out of an old Martin Kane radio script. Graham sat back and waited for Claypoole's reaction.

'I ought to have you tossed in the stockade,' the Colonel said.

'You can't do that to me. I'm a reservist.'

'That's all right,' purred the Colonel. 'There's plenty of room.'

A second later Claypoole was at the door holding it open.

'Let's get one thing straight, Graham. So long as you're in that uniform, you take orders from me. Cross me once, I'll toss you into solitary.'

Graham walked down the corridor a broken man and booming a second behind him came the Colonel's postscript: 'And stay away from the hospital. That's an order, Captain!'

Burnett C. Remington was at war with his soul.

Picture, if you can, 74.5 inches of communications officer driving his jeep into a laundry. A Vietnamese laundry. At lunchtime. Lot of steam. Lot of screams. No one injured but a great deal of detergent turning into bubbles and flowing into the streets of Saigon. Police sirens and military police responding to the spirited denunciation of 'Yankee soldier! Yankee soldier!'

Remington could have stayed and argued his way out of it, but the Colonel would only have found out and forbidden him to drive any more jeeps. Without the jeeps Remington was nothing.

It was all Maxwell's fault, but that was no consolation to Remington. It's one thing to recognize the disease, but to find the cure! In the last few days Remington had known what it meant to fear; to listen for every footstep down mean streets; to distinguish friendly shadows from unfriendlies. Where could a man turn at times like these? Particularly when one's religious views were as widely known as Remington's

It was for all these reasons that Captain Remington found Father Doolan to be such a comfort. The good padre didn't mind Remington not being a Catholic. Unbegrudgingly, the chaplain listened to the Philadelphian's confessions without snitching to anyone.

Remington paused about fifty yards away from Father Doolan's cottage and looked about to see if anyone was in the vicinity. He didn't dare go near the chapel and hoped the kind clergyman would be at home following some amiable pastime.

Hearing what sounded like gunshots from inside the cottage, Remington hesitated for a moment then knocked on the front door. No response. He knocked harder then called out the priest's name. Still no response. Only silence for a few seconds then resumption of the gunshots.

The communications officer kneeled and peeped through the mail slot. On the far wall, he could see a target in the shape of a man. Squinting slightly, he could see that all the bullets had gone straight through the heart. A few seconds later, Father Doolan in shirt sleeves and clerical collar wearing a shoulder holster advanced towards the target area. Remington cleared his throat and called out to him through the mail slot.

'Who is it?' asked Doolan, spinning around aiming his Beretta at the door.

'It is I,' said Remington, over-aware of the formality of his address, 'Captain Burnett C. Remington.'

'What the hell do you want?' asked the priest.

'I want to confess, sir.'

'This isn't a chapel.'

'No, Father Doolan, I know but—'

'Hold on a second!'

Remington assumed the god-man was going to open the door for him, but the latter merely ambled over to the bar, poured himself a stiff shot of whisky, picked up a wicker chair and moved towards the door. Seating himself comfortably, Doolan crossed his right leg over his left, took a sip of his drink, and turned his head towards the mail slot.

'What's the matter, Burnie?'

'Can't I come in?'

Father Doolan ignored the last question and Remington slumped dejectedly down the length of the doorframe. His head was now beside the mail slot.

'Keep talking,' said Doolan.

'I have just driven a jeep into the back of an oriental laundry.'

'That your confession?'

'No, I've cracked up lots of jeeps, Father. I have no moral conflict with that.'

'Fornicating?' asked Doolan hopefully. 'Masturbating?'

'No. Nothing like that.'

'Why not? It'll clear up your skin trouble.'

'I haven't got skin trouble.'

'Anyone with dirty underwear has skin trouble.'

'You promised you wouldn't tease me about that anymore,' wailed Remington.

'Sorry, kid,' snickered Doolan. 'Just cracks me up every time I think of you standing there in front of—'

'Please, please. Let me confess!'

'What is it, for Chrissake?'

Remington swallowed hard then blurted out: 'I confess someone's going to kill me.'

'Burnie,' said the kindly priest, 'you're an imbecile. You can't confess something that hasn't happened. Nor can you confess something passive. You have to have done it. Go kill someone then come and confess.'

'Don't you want to hear about it?'

'Burnie, you're paranoid. I've told you this repeatedly. Find a good psychiatrist and quit bugging me.'

'What kind of a priest are you?' wailed Remington.

'That rhetorical crap'll get you nowhere,' answered the god-man.

'David Maxwell is trying to kill me. He so much as challenged me to a duel yesterday.'

'Did you name your seconds?'

'Of course not.'

'Coward!'

'He'll kill me.'

'How do you know he wasn't bluffing? Maybe he's scared of you. You're a pretty formidable-looking guy. How tall are you?'

'74.5 inches.'

'What is that in cubits?'

'Don't get biblical on me, Father. My soul's at war.'

Doolan uncrossed his legs, then crossed the left one over the right and lit up a Marlboro. Staring nostalgically at the eagle tattooed on his right hand, he withdrew the Beretta from its shoulder holster. He checked the safety catch and replaced the gun under his arm.

'Burnie . . . when's the last time you got laid?'

'Father Doolan!'

'Don't play the outraged virgin with me, Captain. I'm sure you've been a two-backed animal more than once. Take a tumble in the hay. It'll cure you of this fantasy.'

'It isn't a fantasy!'

'It isn't a confession either,' said the god-man. 'It's a supposition. If you're looking for protection, go tell the MP's.'

'I can't. Fowler's in charge. He'll tell the Colonel and the Colonel won't let me drive anymore.'

'He won't let you drive anyhow when he finds out what you did to the jeep,' said Doolan.

The thought had been troubling Remington for hours. He'd been racking his brain to come up with some sort of excuse. But what? He noticed the base newspaper lying on Doolan's doorstep. He scanned the headlines quickly. Something about a bandit.

'I'll simply tell him the truth.' said Remington, trying his lie out on the padre.

'What's that?'

'My car was booby-trapped by Chy Ming's men.'

The front door was suddenly whipped open, and Remington tumbled over into the cottage. No sooner had the captain realized what had happened than he was dragged to his feet by Father Doolan and propped up against the wall with the barrel of the Beretta jammed under his chin.

'What do you know about Chy Ming?' rasped the priest.

Maxwell had his feet up on Edelman's desk when Cashbox appeared—almost magically—in the swivel chair opposite him. She wore a floppy Garbo hat, kooky sunglasses, and a mini skirt something akin to a belt.

'Let's go home,' she said, massaging the inside of his leg with her thumbs and easing up towards his crotch.

'Can't,' said Maxwell, throwing his arms around her to see if she was real and to keep her under control.

He stared down at the beautiful offspring of a casual liaison between a French soldier and an Indo-Chinese shopgirl.

'I thought about you all the time,' she said, staring up into his eyes. 'You really screwed up my holiday.'

'Spur of the moment holiday,' he replied sarcastically.

'Yeah . . . Like my hat?'

'I love the whole outfit. Going to hate taking it off you.'

She tickled the inside of his ear with her tongue.

'No,' she purred. 'You'll sit and watch while I take it off. Come on. Let's go.'

'Cashbox, my ownest own. You've got the world's worst timing. How could you turn up in the middle of the biggest story of the century?'

'Chy Ming?'

'Chy Ming!?'

'Yes. Everyone in the city is talking. Chy Ming has returned to bring peace.'

'Don't tell me you believe that crap.' said Maxwell. 'It's the bloody Viet Cong in paper masks.'

'No, David, it's not the Cong and it's not the black market. They're as amazed as everyone else.'

'Well, who is it?'

'Don't know. But I'm tempted to join him.'

'And give me up?'

'You haven't got any time. Oh, well, you were probably just a whim. . . . Ah! I know what *your* story is.' Cashbox reached for her purse and pulled out a copy of the *New York Times*. 'I brought it from Honolulu. Look. Your old lady.'

The front page featured a photograph of Kip Mendlsohn's funeral. A weeping Sheila Mendlsohn was leaning on Audrey Maxwell's arm.

'Yeah,' murmured Maxwell, 'Said she knew the kid.'

'I hate this war.'

'You and the rest of the world.'

'Not the same. I was born in this war. It had a different name but it was the same war. All my people were born in this war for the past two thousand years. We were born in it and we die in it. Can you describe eternity, David? I can. It's this war. That's why I believe in Chy Ming.'

She reached for her bag and swung it up on her shoulder.

'Where are you going?' asked the correspondent.

'You have no time for me. I'll go and see Doolan.'

'The priest?' laughed Maxwell.

'Don't laugh. He's your rival. You two are the only men who've ever come close to satisfying me.'

'How about dinner? I'll pick you up. You can meet Graham.'

Maxwell watched her walk across the parade ground and delighted in the sheer triumph of her walk. No matter how much clothing she wore she would always be naked. Like a Eurasian Eve walking through a neon Eden. Go on and stare, you poor bastards. She's mine. Or will be once I get *the* story written. Where the hell's Graham? Ah, spoke too soon.

The Murder Man collapsed in the swivel chair and tossed his hat across the room.

'We're in trouble.'

'What's the matter?' asked Maxwell.

'Where do you want me to start?'

'Did you see the kid?'

'Uh-huh. Surly little prick. Doesn't he know he's on trial for his life? He's acting like it's a clerical error they're going to clear up in the morning.'

'What's his story?'

'None. Amnesia or something. Complete blank from when the platoon split up to when he woke up in the hospital. Except for the philgrims.'

'Philgrims? What the hell are philgrims? '

'Spend a day with me sometimes,' said Graham. 'See the bits of information I pick up. I should enter a trivia contest. Do you know what civilian feet are? Colonel Claypoole quizzed me on that.'

'You met Fitzroy.'

'I had the pleasure. He gave me some bullshit story about civilian feet and Chy Ming, whatever that is.'

'Oh, not him, too,' moaned Maxwell. 'Just disregard this Chy Ming business, will you? One of Edelman's circulation boosters. He's trying to sell more papers.'

'Where is Yakov Bak?' the Murder Man asked, referring to the St Louis scribe.

'Went into town to get his laundry. Why?'

'May need him for a little second story work.'

'What's up?'

'Colonel Claypoole and I are not the best of friends.'

Graham proceeded to describe the scar on Tommy Bennett's hand, the possibility Ramirez shot him, and Claypoole's order not to go near the hospital.

'I bloody well can't get near the hospital,' said Maxwell. 'Renfrew will lock me in a straitjacket first chance he gets. No, you're going to have to cable old man Bennett and see if he can get you a promotion.'

'To what?'

'Colonel. Same as Claypoole. A General would be even better.'

'This is the U.S. Army we're talking about, Maxwell, not some coal mine in Wales.'

'What does that mean?'

'Be realistic. This makes great copy for your book but I need a defense ready for the courtroom.'

'You'll never see the courtroom if you end up in the bloody stockade, mate,' said Maxwell, putting a hand on the lawyer's shoulder.

'Don't give me that English "mate" crap,' replied Graham pulling his arm free from the correspondent.

'What's wrong, Frank?'

'I was humiliated today. First by a stupid kid who isn't even grateful I'm trying to save his life. Then by some goddam big-nosed doorman masquerading as a military leader. There's no trial date. Haven't found one defense witness. And I haven't seen my kids in four months.'

Maxwell walked down to the Coca-Cola cooler at the end of the hall and returned with two cokes. He handed one to the Murder Man who murmured a thank you. The correspondent stared at him. The bloke was human after all. Maxwell had never thought of him blowing his cool.

'Why don't you bring your family out here?'

'We're divorced.' said Graham.

Maxwell smiled ironically and pointed to the *Times*: 'That's my wife.'

The lawyer picked up the paper, looked at the picture, and read the caption. 'Handsome woman.'

'We're divorced, too,' added Maxwell.

'Kids?'

'No.' For no reason Maxwell added. 'She was my second wife.'

'I was my wife's second husband. Maybe you should marry my wife. You come from the same background.'

The two men laughed and stared into space for a while.

''Maybe we don't need a medical certificate,' said the correspondent breaking the silence. 'Not if we can get a personal statement from Ramirez. Simply find out whether he shot Bennett or not. And why.'

'Where's Ramirez now? They disbanded the platoon. No way Claypoole will let either one of us near the files.'

'We simply wait for our favorite eager-beaver to return from the laundry,' said Maxwell, positive Edelman would find a way or make it.


Under normal circumstances Harvey Edelman would probably have returned to his office right on cue. It is not a normal circumstance when Captain Remington drives a jeep right into the back end of the laundry where you are waiting for your particular bundle.

What a shmuck! Edelman thought to himself as he saw his gangling superior officer come bursting through the wall. No great surprise. Everyone knew Remington was bound to eventually pull off one colossal lulu of a smashup. Too bad Fingers Mackenzie never lived to see it. He'd always predicted something like that. But Fingers' dream had been for Remington to kill Claypoole and the Montana Cowboys by driving straight into the Cowboys' dugout at the bottom of the ninth inning with a tie score.

Edelman realized he had never covered an accident. Not as an eyewitness. And not with the guilty party running like fury from the scene of the collision. He began to pursue Remington through the back streets of Saigon.

'Stop, soldier! You, soldier, stop!'

All too late, Edelman realized the MPs were shouting after him. Remington was nowhere in sight. Edelman could stop and try to explain but he knew that the military police would bust him up before he got his mouth open. There was nothing to do but catch Remington and get him to confess.

He caught sight of Remington again a few hundred yards away from Father Doolan's cottage. Sanctuary! Edelman had remembered the phrase from the Classics Illustrated version of *The Hunchback of Notre Dame*. The police can't touch him in a church. Did the rule work in a priest's house? This wasn't even a house; it was a cottage. Edelman crept closer.

Confessing! The captain was confessing and he wasn't even a Catholic. Edelman had never really thought about confessing. He liked the basic idea of it. The child-like appeal of saying one was sorry and having anything forgiven. Gee, thought, Edelman, if we could do that it would destroy the Jewish mother forever. Imagine not having to tell her anything because you'd already told the rabbi and he'd forgiven you. Sex! I could have sex and wouldn't go blind or get warts. I could even have sex with my cousin Cynthia in Toledo and wouldn't get in trouble 'cause I'd be forgiven. I want to confess, too, decided Edelman. If Remington can, why not me? Maybe anyone can confess to a Catholic priest. Catholics weren't bad guys after all. They obviously did other things besides getting drunk, beating up their wives, and stoning little Jewish kids on the way home from Hebrew school. Edelman decided he'd confess to Father Doolan as soon as Remington was finished.

Edelman saw the door whipped open and poor Burnett Remington fall into the priest's cottage. Moments later the communications officer fled in panic from the cottage and ran like hell towards the parade ground. Edelman didn't like that part, but he summoned up his courage and decided to have a go at confessing anyways.

Edelman wasn't sure if it was proper to begin the ritual without announcing oneself, so he didn't kneel at the mail slot. Instead, he knocked at the door.

'Who is it?' barked Doolan.

'Harvey Edelman, Father. We've never really spoken, not socially or religiously, but the late Rabbi Goldman always said you were a good golfer and an okay god-man. Rabbi Goldman really felt you were getting your message across— '

'Can the bullshit,' interrupted Doolan. 'What do you want?'

'I want to confess.'

'I can't hear confessions from Jews.'

'Remington's an agnostic.'

'He believes in Ayn Rand.'

Edelman kneeled beside the mail slot and said: 'I believe in Bernard Malamud.'

Something poked Edelman in the nose. The private knew the god-man couldn't possibly have gotten his fist through the mail slot. Then he realized it was the barrel of Father Doolan's Beretta.

'Get out of here, you little prick!' The priest slammed down the flap of the mail slot, but not before the quick-eyed Edelman was convinced he'd seen a naked woman inside the cottage.

Walking along the path back to his office, Edelman weighed various possibilities in his mind. Perhaps Father Doolan was a female impersonator. No. Edelman hadn't seen the naked woman's face, but he had seen one helluva body. The broad-shouldered, burly god-man was obviously breaking his vow of celibacy. But why? Wasn't it obvious? Everyone else could cheat and confess to a priest. Father Doolan was probably only answerable to his mother. He might as well be a Jew.


Cashbox and Maxwell were ordering wine when Graham strode into the restaurant wearing one of his favorite suits. The lawyer was in a particularly good mood and romantically kissed the lady's hand.

'I know now what the war's about,' said Graham, flashing his blue eyes admiringly at Cashbox. The voice had sprung straight from the source of the lawyer's manhood, and he couldn't be responsible for the affect it might have on this unbelievably delectable young woman.

Cashbox rested her chin on her folded hands and smiled warmly at Graham.

'You're full of shit,' she answered, 'but I love your voice.'

My voice! thought Graham. Lady, you've got a voice like a blowjob. A lethal weapon. She's a female me. Please God, don't let her be a lawyer. She'll be on the Carson Show in a flash. She'll have her own series. I've got to marry her quick!

'What do you do here in Saigon?' Graham asked Cashbox, praying his voice wouldn't crack.

Maxwell sank through the floor. He'd forgotten Graham didn't know Cashbox. How could he explain to the Murder Man that this girl wasn't—well, she was. But she wasn't. Not to Maxwell, anyhow. To Maxwell she was—

'I'm a courtesan.'

Maxwell knew he couldn't stare at his spoon all evening. He lifted his head and stared at Graham. Graham stared back at him. The Murder Man didn't know what a courtesan was but he was pretty sure it didn't have anything to do with the law.

'I'm a whore,' said Cashbox, figuring that Graham didn't know what a courtesan was. 'The best damned whore in Saigon.'

Silence followed until Graham asked: 'She's joking, right?'

Maxwell said nothing, having decided he *could* stare at his spoon all evening.

'Do you mind having dinner with a whore?' Cashbox was continuing this theme to get at Maxwell. 'I decided I was going to have a lot of money before I was too old to enjoy it. Like Mr. Sinatra sings: 'Life's been good to me'. Got quite a nest egg. I can retire when I turn twenty-one.'

'She's a minor!' roared Graham.

Maxwell forgot about his spoon and threw his body across the table and stuffed a napkin into Graham's mouth.

'Are you crazy?' hissed Maxwell. 'Want to get us all arrested?'

'Me!?' retorted Graham, pulling the napkin from his mouth. 'I can think of fifteen states you'd be hanged in.'

'Why, Mr. Graham,' Cashbox said sweetly. 'You're a prig.'

'What did she call me?'

'She called you a prig,' said Maxwell. 'And you are. So am I. I'm sorry, Cashbox.'

She took the correspondent's hand and kissed the tips of his fingers.

Graham was still uncomfortable even as the waiter filled Cashbox's wineglass to the top.

'Oh, Murder Man,' said Cashbox. 'Relax. I'm saving the economy. Someone must drink the wine out here. God knows your soldiers won't touch it.'

'It's not bad,' said Graham, taking a sip.

'Oh, it's not the taste,' said Cashbox. 'They don't drink anything anymore. Not since they discovered the marvelous roots and herbs that grow in abundance out here. And to think they used to use hemp for tying knots.'

Graham thought he knew what she meant but wasn't quite sure.

'They're smashed out of their minds, Murder Man. When blue plastic burns and the laser-beam shoots through the night you know marijuana is happening.'

'Isn't that a helluva security risk?' Graham asked naively.

'Bet your life,' winked Cashbox. 'Plenty of stoned cold soldiers walking around on guard duty at night. And on patrols, too. Do you blame them? Fighting an invisible enemy in a war that's never formally been declared. It's a safety valve. Keeps them from deserting but keeps them on the job. They put their heads into limbo. Half the soldiers here are so spaced out you could build a twelve-lane highway through their minds.'

'Why doesn't anyone write about this?' Graham asked, staring at Maxwell.

'No one would print it,' answered the correspondent. 'The repercussions would be fantastic.'

'Yeah,' said Cashbox wistfully, 'it might end the war and that's the last thing anyone wants.'

'Hey, come on,' said Graham.

'It's true,' said Cashbox. 'Ten per cent of the working force in America is involved in the military industrial complex. Can't put those people out of work. Without a war, there's no *raison d'être*. It's just as bad here. The black market won't let you leave. The country would collapse. You've got a hospital ship sitting out there to help our people, but we charge you a fortune to tow the stuff from ship to shore. Then charge you duty for bringing it into the country to save our lives.'

'How do we get out of this mess?' asked Graham.

'We don't,' answered Cashbox. 'My only hope is someone will come along'—Maxwell looked up hopefully— 'and take me to Chy Ming.'

Maxwell groaned: 'You're as bad as everyone else.'

At that moment Captain Remington entered the restaurant. He ate there every Thursday evening 'rain or shine, fire or flood' (you guessed it: F. Claypoole) and this was Thursday evening. Remington was feeling mean. He didn't quite understand what it meant to 'feel mean' but he had come across the word in a Luke Short novel while using the family lavatory in Philadelphia and the phrase had always stayed with him.

He probably felt mean, though, because of the way the day had gone. Driving the jeep into the laundry. Being threatened by Father Doolan. He couldn't understand what had come over the good padre. All he had said was his fib about Chy Ming. Maybe he shouldn't have fibbed. Obviously. As soon as he'd convinced the priest he knew nothing about Chy Ming, the god-man chased him out of the cottage. In his panic to escape from the incensed Father Doolan, Remington was certain he'd seen a naked woman in the bedroom. How the mind plays tricks on us.

That wasn't the end of Remington's troubles. Returning to the office, Colonel Claypoole was waiting for him and 'fit to be tied' (the words were Cleet Fowler's).

Remington didn't know what to tell the Colonel about the jeep. He thought of trying the Chy Ming story again but was afraid the Colonel might pull a gun on him or, worse, turn him over to Fowler. Maybe he should simply go down on his hands and knees and beg his forgiveness.

'Please, sir—'

'Get up off your knees, Captain. You'll soil your uniform.'

Remington didn't like Claypoole's choice of words. But he rose from his knees anyhow.

'Think I'll call Sergeant Fowler in here.'

'No, please, sir.'

'Let go of my sleeve, you whimpering coward, and answer one question.'

Remington felt the Colonel was unnecessarily hard about one cracked-up jeep and a dented oriental laundry. But that's why Remington was a captain and Claypoole was a colonel. These were the facts of life one wasn't taught at the Point.

'What the hell are "civilian feet"?'

Remington said nothing. The Colonel stuffed the memo in his face.

'This is your writing, isn't it, Captain? What does it mean?'

'I can't remember, sir.' He really couldn't.

'You're in it with them, aren't you? You Judas! I ought to turn you over to Sergeant Fowler but killing's too good for you. . . . You're from an old army family, aren't you, Remington? How would they feel about a dishonorable discharge?'

Remington, to quote the late Ralph Rolingo, didn't know whether to shit, go blind, or wind his watch. Claypoole had been correct. A discharge would be worse than death to him. What was he to do? There was some consolation in the Colonel not knowing about the laundry. Wait a minute! Why not use the excuse for the jeep to get out of this 'civilian feet' business.

'Wasn't sure whether intelligence had briefed you, sir,' said Remington, diving in headfirst, 'but it has to do with Chy Ming, the bandit.'

If Colonel Claypoole had dentures in his mouth, they would have crashed to the floor.

'There *is* a Chy Ming?'

'Does the Colonel have reason to believe there isn't?' asked Remington, completely committed to his lie.

'Why wasn't I told?'

'It was in the paper, sir.'

The Colonel couldn't argue with that. Edelman had been right for once. Good boy Edelman! He'd speak to him in the morning about—oh, no! Graham. He had betrayed a piece of intelligence to Graham. He had told him there was a definite link between Chy Ming and 'civilian feet'. Graham probably told Maxwell. And Maxwell told the world.

'We've got to do something,' murmured the Colonel.

'Possibly a search-and-destroy mission to find this bandit and smoke him out of his lair,' suggested Remington, who was now thoroughly enjoying his fantasy.

'Like the Wichita Platoon?' the Colonel retorted bitterly. Wait a minute! That's it! Might be the answer to everything. Even Santiago couldn't have come up with Claypoole's brainwave. There would be no trial. No publicity. Nothing. The entire blame could be laid at Chy Ming's feet. The unfortunate Wichita Ball Club had been brutally massacred by the mountain bandit.

'But we know that's not true, sir,' said Remington.

'Do we, Captain? *I* know nothing of the sort. You'd be advised not to know anything either. Don't want your picture on the cover of *Time* and *Newsweek*, do you?'

It had always been a dream of Burnett Remington's to be on the covers of *Time* and *Newsweek* but not on charges of perjury and conspiracy. Security blanket that the bandit story had been, he had to tell the truth.

'Sir, there is no Chy Ming.'

'What?'

'Sorry, sir. It's a story of Edelman's. Thought I'd use it as an excuse because I drove a jeep into the back of a laundry at lunchtime.'

'Then what are "civilian feet"?' asked a bewildered and shattered Claypoole.

Remington still didn't know but replied with a simple and logical: 'They're the opposite of military feet.'

'Why did you want to speak to me about them?'

'We never talk anymore.'

The Colonel got up and walked to the window. He had never hated anyone as much in his life as he did Remington at that moment. Even when he'd fought the Germans, he hadn't really hated them. But he sincerely wanted to destroy Remington. Fowler could do it but that would be too quick. Cleet-boy knew nothing of sophisticated torture. The Colonel knew he could never have Remington court martialed. Not for telling the truth. No, he'd have to keep Remington in the service but crippled. He would forbid him to drive jeeps.

Remington returned to his quarters and cried for the first time since he was a child.

Then he remembered it was Thursday. He pulled himself together and took a humiliating taxi to the restaurant.

When he stepped into the restaurant and saw Graham one could well appreciate what a logical target for Remington's spleen the Murder Man was. Captain Graham wasn't wearing his uniform. He was in civilian dress without permission. The communications officer strode across the floor of the restaurant.

'Have you written permission to be in civvies, Captain?' asked the Philadelphia martinet.

'Piss off,' said Maxwell.

Remington's lip began to tremble. 'I wasn't addressing you, Mr. Maxwell.' Remington's heart was pounding.

'He's the same rank as you,' said Maxwell contemptuously.

Remington emitted a scream and grabbed a fork.

'Stay away from me!' shrieked Remington. 'You don't frighten me. I know how to use this. Don't provoke me. Life may not be important to you, and I might be another name on a forgotten list but I won't die without a fight. Stay where you are!'

Everyone stared at the extremely tall, deranged soldier as he backed his way out of the restaurant holding a fork in his right hand and shielding his face with his left. Dropping his guard to reach for the door handle, Remington disappeared into the night.

'Another casualty,' said Cashbox, shaking her head sadly.

Graham excused himself after the meal and took a cab back to his hotel leaving Maxwell and Cashbox alone. She had long-before removed her shoes and now glided a stockinged left-foot between his legs under the table and began to arouse him with her toes.

'God, you make it hard,' he said.

'Double entendre?'

'Yeah, but I meant difficult. Must be up at seven. Frank and I have a lot of work to do.'

'All work and no play,' she said soothingly.

'Raincheck?' asked Maxwell,

'I thought something special was happening to us, David. Maybe I was wrong.'

'Cashbox—'

'My name isn't Cashbox. Not since this afternoon.'

'What happened this afternoon?'

'Goodbye, David.'

The Wichita Ball Club's beloved hooker-goddess walked out of the restaurant and grabbed the nearest cab.

Half an hour later she was undressing in Father Doolan's cottage.

# *THE ELUSIVE SURVIVORS*

'Get yourself a new boy, Yang.'

'Harvey, what are you talking about?'

'Father Doolan.'

'Tell me later, Harvey, the briefing is going to start any minute now.'

It was the first official press briefing since Maxwell dropped the initial bomb about the quarantine. Policy since then had been strictly every man for himself. With the arrival of Major Walter Dundas, the army lawyer, and the announcement of the trial date certain concessions had to be made.

Nearly eight hundred newsmen pressed into the recreation hall. Colonel Claypoole was to introduce Dundas to the correspondents and dispense additional information about the trial.

Graham hadn't felt this sort of uneasiness since his law exams fifteen years earlier. He was irritated with Maxwell for not having shown up yet. Probably still rolling around in the hay with his teenage hooker. Now Edelman was trying to cloud his mind with some mumbo-jumbo about the Catholic chaplain. Where did the kid get his energy from? Probably no sex life. Not that Graham had gotten off the nut in the past five weeks. Should have screwed Miss Cable before he left the office. Probably never see her again. Or would he? No time to get horny. Gazing into the rec hall, he saw Colonel Claypoole step up onto the platform.

'Harvey, quick! Give me your pad and pencil. I don't know where Maxwell is, so I have to take notes.'

'What about me?' squawked Edelman.

'I've got your back. There are more important things you need to do. While old Fitzroy does his spiel, get over to the admin office and find out where the rest of the Wichita Platoon is. Maxwell and I can't do it. You're our only hope.'

Edelman's chest expanded at least six inches. The torch had been passed. He'd been asked to raise the flag on Iwo Jima. To be the first man to hit Omaha Beach. His two heroes couldn't do it but *he* could.

'Yes, sir,' said Edelman, saluting smartly and heading towards the administration building.

Walking down the aisle towards the front of the rec hall, Graham heard murmurs of recognition from the press corps. He wanted to sit close for a good look at Dundas, a stocky, middle-aged African American.

Barry Lomax waved to him from the fifth row.

'Hi, Barry,' said Graham sitting down beside the Australian journalist. The two had known each other casually since the Rizitski case.

'Love your uniform,' smiled Lomax.

'Shut up,' said Graham good-naturedly. He pointed to the platform. 'Himself is about to speak.'

'Good morning, gentlemen,' intoned Claypoole. 'Glad you could all be here this morning at this early hour. Sharing the joy of the worm.'

Lomax turned to Graham and asked: 'Is he drunk?'

'No, he says things like that. First week I was here he came up with: "The work of a hoe is not helped by a ho." Turned it into a poster and stuck it up on every wall on the base.'

'I have called you here this morning,' continued the Colonel, 'to introduce Major Walter Dundas, who will be representing the army in the hearing that will commence in a week's time.'

All the correspondents started writing the information down furiously. Graham simply wrote the word HEARING in block letters then underlined it several times.

'This hearing will determine the validity of certain allegations that have been rife around this base and in the foreign press for several weeks now.'

Graham now drew a box around the word HEARING and tied a string to the box connecting it to a balloon containing an emphatic Shit!

'What's the matter?' whispered Lomax in his thick Aussie accent.

'A hearing is not a trial. Claypoole is slipping it to us again. He knows I can't summon witnesses to a hearing. But I *can* subpoena them for a trial.'

Having completed the official statement that he had summoned the press to hear, the Colonel generously offered five minutes for the press to ask any questions that they wanted. The questioning began. Safe, boring, and predictable.

Graham used the question-and-answer period to size up Major Walter Dundas.

He needed to hear Dundas speak, but Claypoole was hogging all the answers. Dundas didn't seem to mind. He sat on the platform with a curious smile on his face staring out almost insolently at the assembled members of the press. Graham immediately loved and hated the man. One part of him prayed Dundas had a lousy voice. The other part hoped for a worthy vocal adversary. He wished he didn't have to go up against Dundas. He'd like to go for a drink with him instead. Talk to him. Find out why he was an army lawyer instead of out in the big time. Probably does have a lousy voice. Why else would he bury himself in the army? Funny the army not bringing in a big gun to face Graham. Maybe the African American Dundas *was* their big gun. Graham wasn't an aficionado of great post-war military trials. Maybe Dundas was a legal titan whom the army was forcing to represent them. Maybe he had a contract he couldn't break. What Dundas needed was a good lawyer. Graham decided he would send him to see Bochner when the trial was over.

The Murder Man looked at his pad again and saw the box with the word HEARING inside. There would be no trial. The case was going to fizzle out in an interminable hearing. Maxwell must have known that. No wonder he wasn't there. It wasn't *the* story. And if it wasn't *the* story it wasn't *the* case either. Everyone was wasting their goddam time. On a stupid hearing with no witnesses. Because you can't have witnesses without a trial. But . . . on the other hand, you can't have a trial without witnesses. Graham! Fool! That's it! No one knows about the witnesses, or they simply haven't bothered to ask. Like Maxwell and the quarantine. Someone has to get the ball rolling. Where was Maxwell? Graham looked around the room. He now regretted having sent Edelman off to the administration building. Well, there was no other way.

'Colonel, I'd like to ask a question.'

'Captain Graham, questions are intended for the members of the working press. You aren't even supposed to—'

'Could someone please tell me what happened to the surviving members of the Wichita Platoon?'

'Captain, you're out of line,' said Claypoole with the word STOCKADE blazing from his eyes.

'I'd like to answer the captain's question.'

All eyes in the recreation hall suddenly focused on Major Dundas, who had spoken for the first time that morning. It was the voice of a basso profundo. Graham's heart sank.

'Most of you gentlemen are all too aware of the unfortunate repercussions that can occur when too much advance publicity is given to a case.' Dundas paused cleverly to allow the past transgressors recall their transgressions. 'There have already been too many instances here in South-East Asia of needless and biased interrogation of witnesses, potential witnesses, and the publication of what they say before it is said in court. The army wishes to avoid this at all costs in this case. If there are surviving members of the platoon, who can offer constructive testimony we will be more than willing to hear them. But we have not and will not allow them to be badgered and hounded by unscrupulous reporters, who only bring shame on their fellow members of an honorable profession.'

Dundas' answer-cum-speech was greeted by an unprecedented and thunderous round of applause by the newsmen.

'Now, Gentlemen,' said Dundas, picking up his attaché case, 'that satisfactorily concludes the briefing.'

The Major left the platform followed by a stunned Colonel Claypoole, who had never been so up staged in his career (even when a famous starlet lost her top in the middle of a USO tour). Lomax and the other veteran reporters were trying to obtain off-the-record statements from the velvet-tongued prosecutor.

A solitary Frank Graham was left behind in the recreation hall. Alone and afraid. He was frightened of Dundas. Not just his Paul Robeson voice but the words he used. The affect was overwhelming. Charisma Incorporated. Dundas walked into the briefing a stranger and emerged an idol. Graham even felt a bit sorry for Claypoole but not as sorry as he was feeling for himself.

Allowing himself to wallow in self-pity for another thirty seconds, he decided something extraordinary had to be done. Frank Graham was fighting for his life. Jacob about to wrestle with the Angel. If he won the struggle, he need never look back again.

Something else about the briefing had bothered Graham. Not a major irritation like the use of the word 'hearing'. Something that was missing. Not something but someone. Where was Captain Remington? Why hadn't he been on the platform? What happened to the communications officer after he fairbanksed his way out of the restaurant? Maybe the whole fork business had been an act. There was no reason for him to fear Maxwell. Of course, it was an act. Another ploy of Claypoole's. Convince them Remington was cracking up. Have him stay away from the briefing so their consciences would bother them. It's not going to work, Claypoole. Takes a better man than you to scare off Frank Graham.

'Hi, Frank.'

Graham gazed up at Maxwell. The correspondent was a mess.

'Where have you been?' demanded Graham. 'You look terrible.'

'Haven't slept.'

'Couldn't get enough, eh?'

'I didn't "get" any, thank you very much. Been up all night searching for her. Checked her apartment, hotel, and embassy in Saigon. No trace of her. She's vanished, Frank. Vanished.'

'That's impossible.'

'It is not unprecedented.'

'Want some coffee?' asked Graham.

'I've had 55 cups in the last twelve hours. Going to pee bloody Maxwell House for the next fortnight. What am I going to do, Frank?'

'Forget her.'

'Easy for you to say. She's the only thing I've got to live for.'

'Wanna bet? How about Claypoole not having a trial but opting out for a hearing that'll flush your story down the toilet?'

'What!!' Color returned abruptly to Maxwell's face. The will to live had returned. 'He can't do that to us. The world has a right to know the truth. I've got to tell them.'

'Attaboy!'

'What are we going to do?' He rubbed his hands together maniacally. He was punchy from lack of sleep. 'What are we going to do, Frank?'

'We've got to find Harvey.'

'Has Harvey vanished, too?'

'Let's hope not,' smiled Graham.

'We're going to be all right, aren't we, Frank?'

There was an almost child-like quality in the correspondent's request. It made Graham feel important. This was his show. Exit the correspondent. Enter the Murder Man.

Enter Harvey Edelman, who caught up with his two heroes walking along a pathway.

'I found them!' shouted Edelman, waving some pieces of paper in his hand. 'I found them!'

'What's he saying?' asked a doddering Maxwell, whose childishness had now shifted into senility.

'It's all right, David,' said Graham, squeezing the correspondent's hand. 'He's found the Wichita Platoon.'

Found, yes. But accessibility was another question. Seven had been discharged from the service. Four had been transferred to Germany.

'We're still wiped out,' said Graham.

'One left,' smiled Edelman. 'Ramirez. He's on R&R leave in Honolulu.'

'Harvey, you're a great man.'

If he'd had been given the Legion of Honor, it wouldn't have meant more than Frank Graham's words. Harvey Edelman had finally arrived. Ten years after his bar-mitzvah, he'd become a man. And a great one at that.

'Before I forget,' said Edelman, 'Something else I found out at the admin building. Captain Remington has vanished. He didn't come back to the officers' quarters last night.'

Maxwell stared at Graham. 'Get out of that uniform, Frank.'

'What are you talking about?'

'You have three alternatives: demotion, promotion, or getting out of that uniform. Sooner or later every species vanishes. Right here. This is my Galapagos. I've seen it happen. Survival of the fittest. I've watched them all vanish. Platoons, doctors, Quonset huts, hookers. Now captains. You're doomed if you stay in that uniform!'

Maxwell had grown quite vocal by this time, so Graham and Edelman took him behind a bush to try and calm him down.

'You're tired. David. You've got to get some rest so you can go to Honolulu and find Ramirez.'

'Ramirez has vanished.'

'No. Harvey found him.'

'Then let Harvey go get him.'

'Harvey can't go wherever he wants. You can.'

'I won't vanish?'

'You can't,' said Graham. 'You're a correspondent. You must tell the story. You'd be the last one to vanish.'

Maxwell thought about it and seemed calmer.

Edelman drew Graham aside. 'Will he be all right?'

'Yeah, yeah. Just needs some sleep.'

'Remember what I was saying before?' asked Edelman. "Get yourself a new boy, Yang."'

'How could I forget?'

'It's from a Humphrey Bogart picture.' explained Edelman. 'Bogart's a mercenary working for a Chinese war lord named Yang, who he runs away from. That's when he says: "Get yourself a new boy, Yang."'

'Does this story go someplace?' asked Graham impatiently.

'Father Doolan. There's something funny about him.'

'Like what?'

'He has a Beretta.'

'All priests have birettas.'

'No! A bang-bang Beretta.'

'Harvey, do you realize what you're saying? This isn't Terry and the fuckin' Pirates with Chopstick Joe and the Dragon Lady. You're talking about a man of God.'

'I saw it,' insisted Edelman. 'He stuck it in my nose yesterday through the mail slot. And that's not all I saw. He had a naked woman in there.'

'Harvey, were you stoned?'

'No, sir. Drove me crazy all afternoon. I went back at night and watched the cottage. Nothing happened. Until midnight, when a taxi pulled up and she got out.'

'Who?'

'Cashbox. Father Doolan's been screwing Cashbox.'

Something akin to the sound of a wounded tiger was heard and Maxwell flew at Edelman's throat. It took all of Graham's strength to pull him off the kid.

'I'll kill him!' wailed Maxwell. 'I'll kill him!'

'Stop it, David!'

Graham hit his collaborator across the face.

The three sat behind the bush for several minutes breathing heavily.

'Thought she was making it up,' Maxwell finally murmured. 'It can't be true. Harvey, are you sure?'

'Positive.'

'Swear to me on the memory of John Garfield that everything you said was true.'

'I saw everything I said I did, Mr. Maxwell.'

'You actually saw her—With him?'

'Well, not *doing* it—'

'Aha! So, you don't know.'

'I waited till four in the morning, Mr. Maxwell. She didn't come out.'

'I told you to forget her,' said Graham. 'Come on. You've got to find Ramirez.'


Fitzroy Claypoole posted a triple guard around the gymnasium, put on his best lavender sweat suit, then set about the task of physical fitness. He couldn't stand working out with the other men. His body was a private affair and how he used it and developed it was no one's business but his own.

He bounded over the vaulting horse three times and tried to forget his problems, but the images continued to flash in front of him. He tried rowing them away but as he pulled strenuously on the oars he kept seeing Dundas in the bow of the boat. He shouldn't let the Major bother him. The man was simply there to do a job and leave. What if he didn't leave? He could stage a coup and took over the base. That colored man had charisma. The men would follow him anywhere. Even Cleet-boy. His boy. Involved in the first American junta. Where *was* the grizzly bear? Claypoole had sent for him a half hour before. Why was he late? Perhaps the junta was in power already. Circumstances couldn't be better. The base commander under triple guard by his own order. A perfect scenario. Claypoole had greased the wheels of disaster himself. Served the base up to Dundas on a silver platter. They were probably coming for him any second. How would they do it? Not hanging! They wouldn't debase him by hanging. He'd insist on a firing squad. It was only fitting. He'd given thirty years of his life to the service. The least they could give him was a firing squad. What would his final words be? After refusing a blindfold, of course. Something they would always remember. How about: 'A little part of me will always be in that bullet.' Hmm. Clearly on the right track. More like: 'You cannot kill me with anything I have loved more.' No. Relied too much on the past. There should be the promise of Valhalla as an inspiration to others. Perfect! 'I have served the eagle all my life. Now I will fly with it.'

Claypoole said the proposed epitaph aloud a few times and liked the sound of it. Walking about the gymnasium, he rolled the words off his lips.

Let them come! Let them find me here. I will not be unprepared. They shan't take me without a struggle. But what to struggle with? It would have to be the basics. None of the modern mechanics of war. Looking around the gym, his eyes fell on the Indian clubs. Indian clubs! The very words conjured up images of early America. The first cold winters. Hand-to-hand combat. Man against the elements with only the god Mars as his companion. Claypoole removed the Indian clubs from their rack and poised himself behind the vaulting horse. He was ready.

Nothing happened for five minutes. Then he heard heavy footsteps from outside. This was it! He gripped the first Indian club in his right hand and drew his arm back. Unable to calculate the number he might hurl before they stopped him, he'd make every one count until they did. The door budged slightly then swung open. Claypoole fired his first Indian club.

It hit Cleet Fowler square on the forehead and knocked the Montana sergeant unconscious.

The Colonel leaped over the vaulting horse and ran to the fallen sergeant. He cradled the grizzly bear's head in his arms.

Fowler slowly opened his eyes and asked: 'Wha'd you do that for, Pa?'

'Forgive me, boy,' said Claypoole, tears forming in his eyes. 'It's the war.'

'Whatcha talkin' 'bout?'

'Hasn't Dundas taken over the base?'

'Hell, no!' said Fowler, getting up on his feet and rubbing his forehead. 'Gonna have a big lump.'

'Best steak, Cleet-boy. The best steak there is.'

'You all right, boss?'

The switch from 'pa' to 'boss' did not go unnoticed by the Colonel. He gripped the Sergeant's arm.

'Sorry, boy.'

'It's okay, Pa. Take more'n an old Injun club to stop me.'

Fowler let out a hoot of delight and the Colonel joined him.

'Had me worried there for a while, Pa.'

'Me too,' said Claypoole. Then he paused for a second. 'The reason I sent for you, Cleet-boy. I know how you're always trying to surprise me. Doing things you think I'll like. And I appreciate it. You know that. So, I was just wondering . . . Have you done something with Captain Remington?'

'Hell, no.'

'Sure?'

'What's the matter, Pa?'

'I can't find him, Cleet-boy. Looked all over the base. Not like Remington to vanish. Gutless worm that he is, he's no deserter. That's why I thought you . . .'

'I got nothin' 'gainst Burnie. 'Cept his drivin'. Y'know he busted up a laundry yesterday?'

'Hmm. I told him he couldn't drive anymore.'

'Ya shouldn't have done that, Pa. Ya probably broke his heart and he's lying dead somewhere. Maybe ran off with that jezebel. Ya know. That there hooker. The one they call Cashbox. She's gone, too. The Englishman's been looking for her day and night. No sign of her anywhere. Maybe they eloped.'

Claypoole snorted at Fowler's romanticism: 'Remington wouldn't know what end to put it in.'

'Good riddance to 'em both,' concluded Fowler.

'Easy for you to say, Cleet-boy. What am I going to do for a communications officer? I had a cable from Washington after the briefing today. Santiago's going to be here in three days to supervise the hearing.'

'Lemme be the c'munications officer,' said Fowler.

The proposal was out of the question. Fowler could neither read nor write. On second thought, thought Claypoole, it wasn't such a bad idea. There'd be no problem with paperwork. He'd give Fowler a chance.

Graham decided he couldn't wait an extra day, so he poured Maxwell onto the first available transport bound for Hawaii. The Englishman could sleep on the plane and wake up fit to follow through his investigations. In the meantime, Graham would bring as much possible pressure to bear to have Tommy Bennett tried by a general court martial. Possibly he could goad Dundas into it.

Maxwell got a few hours' sleep on the plane and felt better upon his arrived in Honolulu. Even managed a healthy phallic response when the pretty *malihini* put a *lai* around his neck at the airport. She must have realized what had occurred for she giggled immediately.

'Tell me your name,' said Maxwell, trying to cover up the first flush of blush.

'Luana.'

Maxwell checked his watch. He hadn't switched it from Saigon time, but he knew there wasn't time enough. *Goodbye, Luana. I will always love you. The cleanest looking girl I've ever seen in my life.*

The correspondent parked his bag in the hotel then began searching for Corporal Jaime Ramirez. Edelman had given him a list of hotels servicemen stayed at for their rest and recreation leaves. Maxwell had gone down four on the list before discovering the one where Ramirez was registered. The room clerk thought the corporal was probably out on the beach.

The warm, white sand spilled into Maxwell's shoes as he stepped over nubile and fecund bikinis in his search for the Mexican American. *Why the hell hadn't Edelman given him a picture of Ramirez? Nine million people were on the beach that afternoon and all seemed to be lovely, tanned dollies with that anxious look in their eyes. Nine million women for every man. They all looked so clean. No time. No time. Nine million dollies and I'm looking for a man. What if they'd got to him already? The anxious ones. He's probably lying somewhere out there amidst that mass of breasts, legs, and what-nots. One burnt-out Mexican carcass. Get a lot of information out of that.*

Farther down the beach Maxwell came across a party of six girls. As he stepped in front of them their eyes lit up. They got off their beautiful bottoms and started jumping up and down waving lustfully at the same time. Maxwell had never seen such an exhibition of predatory passion in his life. At that moment he was ready to forget *the* case and *the* story and offer himself up as a human sacrifice to these bronzed, lithe Amazons.

'Jaime! Jaime!'

It wasn't Maxwell who held the girls' interest. No. Their attention was focused on the short, handsome Latino surfing towards them.

The young man glided his surfboard in neatly, tucked it under his arm, and jogged back up the beach. The girls greeted him with an enthusiasm bordering on nympholepsy.

Maxwell had found his man. 'Corporal Ramirez?'

'*Si*—Yes.'

'My name is David Maxwell and—'

'Senor Maxwell! What an honor. Girls, please. Not now. Don't touch there!' He swore at them affectionately in Spanish and turned to Maxwell: 'They are like little children. They love to touch.'

'Maybe they think it's a good luck charm,' muttered Maxwell. 'Can I speak to you alone?'

'Of course,' said Ramirez in heavily accented English. '*Chiquitas*, split! Later. Oooh! *Puta*!!'

One of the girls made a last desperate grab at his bathing suit.

'That Meredith,' laughed Ramirez, 'she is very playful. Yesterday she get my bathing suit away from me in the water. Funny girls, no?'

'Who are they?'

'Students from University of Miami. They come for the sun.'

'Corporal—'

'Call me Jaime.'

'Okay,' smiled Maxwell. 'Is there somewhere we can talk?'

'Why not here?' suggested Ramirez, stretching out on the sand. 'Take off your shirt. Get some sun.'

Maxwell removed his shirt, shoes, and socks. The warm sand felt good under his toes.

'Jaime, where have you been for the last three weeks?'

'Yesterday I go to pineapple factory. Very interesting but—'

'Let's start again,' suggested Maxwell, realizing one couldn't streamline things with the Mexican Apollo. 'How long have you been here?'

'Two weeks.'

'Two weeks!?! R&R isn't supposed to be for more than five days.'

'Yes. They are very good to me. Says on my pass: Unlimited Time. Old Claypoole is one okay guy.'

Two weeks. Something was wrong with the chronological order. The whole business hadn't started more than three weeks before. The Quonset hut had only been gone for three days. The light at the end of the tunnel was extinguished.

'How long were you in the Quonset hut?'

'Quonset hut?' asked Ramirez, not understanding the word.

'The large aluminum structure in the jungle,' explained Maxwell.

'Oh, *si*. Three days. For observation.'

'Who did the observing?'

'No one,' answered Ramirez. 'They say they observe. But they don't. I ask them when I go for observe.'

'Did anyone else ask?'

'No. They say mind my own business. Why they say that to me, Mr. Maxwell?'

'Did they let you all out at once?' asked Maxwell, ignoring Ramirez' question.

'No. Just me. In the middle of the night, Captain Remington comes to my bunk in the— how you call it? —Quonset hut and tells me get dressed. I go on R&R.'

'Did they give you any special instructions?' asked the correspondent. He couldn't understand how Claypoole had been foolish enough to let the talkative Ramirez into the outside world.

'No. Sergeant Fowler drive me to airfield, give me box of balloons and says: "Get some "poontang".'

'Weren't they worried about your reading the newspapers?'

Ramirez paused at this question and grew slightly embarrassed. He took a breath.

'I speak English pretty good. But still not read it much. Better than Fowler. But this is better than none.'

'Don't you know about the platoon?'

'Señor Maxwell. I am confused. I want to be citizen. They say if I go in army, it will happen more quick. I join army and soon they make me corporal. I have friends and I play baseball. Damn good second baseman. No shit. They tease me about grapes. But I understand that is their way. They no understand because they are not there. But we are good *amigos*. Then this thing happens and I do not understand. No one explains to me. I worry I do wrong. No one says nothing. "Shut up, spic!" says Sergeant Grocowicz. I call him dumb Polack and we fight. Tell him I want to be observe. Captain Remington comes in the night and tells me I go here.'

Maxwell rolled over on his stomach and poked at the sand. He wondered what it would be like to be buried in the stuff and let the tide come in. He thought of Brighton as a child. Sunday on the pier and a penny to see what the butler saw. He thought of Helena for the first time in years. How had she made out with her bloke from the Inland Revenue? Were they terribly happy in their terribly nice home in terribly suburban Putney? Were there children? Children who might have been Maxwell's if he had stuck around. They might all be in Brighton now enjoying the sun surrounded by a marvelous wall of water. With no central heating, a phone that occasionally worked and Guinness spilling all over one's shirt in the local. Anything but this goddam war.

'Tell me what happened in the jungle,' said Maxwell.

'We get orders on Thursday go on patrol. Search and destroy. What they call it now? "Protective reaction." *Si*. On Friday morning, we go. All twenty of us. Rolingo complains after ten minutes. Pack hurts. Feets hurt. He is thirsty. Fingers gets idea for pack with gas in it. How you call it? Helium? Keep everything up. He will make fortune. This Fingers, always makes fortune. Always go to Keller for advice. Some business heads, those two. . .. We stop in afternoon. Grocowicz makes us into three. He takes five. I take five. Mendlsohn takes six. Tommy stays behind to watch equipment and set up radio. I gone two hours. We find nothing. It rains so I go back. When we get near, I hear shooting. Machine gun. I run forward. I see Tommy. I do not believe what I see. I think it is dream. I raise my gun. . ..'

'Then you *did* shoot Bennett?'

'I must, *señor*. I wanted to stop him before— but it was too late. They were all dead when I got there.'

'What did you use to shoot Tommy?'

'My pistol. I only want wound him. When you shoot machine gun is hard to stop.'

'Who have you told this story to, Jaime?'

'No one. Grocowicz comes soon after. I say we should radio. He say it would start a panic. He say there is too much scandal. We go back to base.'

'What about the—the bodies?'

'Grocowicz say leave them. Someone comes for them later.'

'How did you get to the Quonset hut?'

'We do not go right to base. We stop a few miles outside and Grocowicz goes ahead. He comes back an hour later and tells us we camp there two days. We do this. On Sunday, they move us into the Quonset hut.'

'Didn't you think this was strange?'

'They say they want observe us.'

'For what?'

The look on Ramirez's face registered the fact he never really understood what 'observe' meant. Simply that it hadn't happened.

'Where was Bennett during all this?'

'I guard him.'

'Did he say anything?'

'He was loco. I bandage his hand after I shoot him. He says nothing. Sort of smiles. Like at funeral.'

'How do you mean loco?' Maxwell knew there was no sense introducing terms like schizophrenic or psychotic.

'Not crazy-loco. Mushroom-loco. Stoned. You know? High.'

'Are you sure?'

'I see some stoned cold soldiers but never like this one.'

'Did he talk on the way back?'

'Nothing. I don't think Tommy know where he is. That night he cries. He don't stop. Grocowicz give him some kind of pill and he sleep. In the morning he gone. Grocowicz say MPs took him in the night.'

Maxwell looked at his watch and wondered when he could get a plane back to Saigon. Graham would need this information as soon as possible. The correspondent started to put his shoes on.

'Jaime, are you willing to tell all this in court? They can subpoena you anyhow.'

'Yes. I want to tell. Is not right no one knows.'

'My sentiments exactly. Keep stumm till you hear from me. Don't say anything to anyone. Just keep getting your poontang. That should keep you busy enough.'

'Please, Señor Maxwell. What is poontang?'

'The University of Miami,' answered the correspondent gesturing down the beach.

'Ahhh!' said Ramirez with a knowing smile and a healthy wink. 'What do I do with balloons?'

'You don't need them.'

To safeguard against Ramirez starting the trend towards vanishing Mexicans, Maxwell typed up a statement and had the Corporal sign it. With the document tucked safely in his pocket, he caught the night flight to Saigon.


'We're in business,' said Maxwell, bursting into Graham's bedroom and waving the document.

Graham squinted and reached for his cigarettes on the night table. He managed to find his mouth and got a match there without burning his lips.

'Didn't think you wore pajamas,' said the correspondent as he watched Murder Man shrug himself into a state of consciousness.

'I do when I sleep alone . . . What is that?'

'A statement from Ramirez. He shot Bennett all right. Unfortunately, it was a preventive measure. Too late. Afraid Tommy did it.'

'I know,' said Graham glumly. 'Went to see my client today. A changed man. Surliness has vanished. He's very humble. Kind of pleasant. Kind of vague. Wants to help any way he can. And he's more than willing to admit he killed them.'

# THE WHITE HOUSE WATCHDOG

Graham scrutinized the document Maxwell handed him. It seemed to back up the Murder Man's theory of the previous day. Tommy Bennett was another stoned cold soldier. Which explained his new humility and vagueness. He was taking the easy way out.

'How's he getting the stuff into the stockade?' asked Maxwell.

'Maybe Edelman can tell us.'

'Where is Harvey?' asked Maxwell.

'He's in the stockade.'

'What!?'

'Claypoole threw him in for blasphemy.'

Maxwell sat down for that one. Gone less than twenty-four hours and he'd missed an entire reel of the movie. In less than a day Thomas Jefferson Bennett had freaked out under an armed guard and Harvey Edelman was doing a remake of *The Fixer*. What else?

'Chy Ming blew up a bridge,' answered Graham.

'Frank, for Chrissake, there is no Chy Ming.'

'There is, David. That's the final irony. There is a Chy Ming and everyone's after him. The black market is offering a reward for his capture. The Cong want him dead. And the Army wouldn't be unhappy if a couple of grenades went off in his pocket. This war's the only game in town and they have to set a limit on the number of shooters.'

'Thank God, we don't have to worry about him,' said the correspondent.

'Says who? He could be the prosecution's scapegoat. If they claim he did it, the whole case goes out the window. I'm not saying they are going to do it but we've got to be ready for any eventuality.'

'Why do you blaze your blue eyes at me when you say 'we'?' asked Maxwell.

'*I* won't be able to find Chy Ming,' replied the Murder Man.

Maxwell was in no mood to discuss his newly acquired status of being Frank Graham's leg man, so he decided to switch the topic.

'How did Harvey get tossed in the stockade?'

'Defending your honor,' explained Graham. 'Or something like that. The kid idolizes you, David, and when you cracked up yesterday—

'I didn't crack up!'

'Whatever you were doing behind that bush yesterday when you tried to strangle Harvey, he forgave you for it. He was prepared to go to any lengths to remove the doubts from your mind. He went to see Claypoole and told him what he saw. Claypoole sent for Doolan, who denied everything. Harvey made a scene. Brought up the naked woman. That's when Claypoole charged him with blasphemy and threw him in the stockade.'

'Who does Claypoole think he is?' demanded the correspondent. 'You can't charge a Jew with blasphemy. Have you tried getting him released?'

'Oh, sure. On top of preparing my defense and having nightmares about Dundas, it's all I've been doing with my spare time. Harvey isn't putting up that much of a fuss.'

'No, I suppose it's a wish fulfilment for him. Carrying his cross or Star of David. He probably makes a good contact man on the inside.  Think I can visit him?'

'You're listed as next of kin.'

'Really?' asked Maxwell, quite touched by Edelman's lie.

Harvey Edelman lay on his cot and took it all in. He was a prisoner. Fantastic! He was turning into one helluva guy. Twenty-three-years-old and he was in the can. In stir. Locked in the hoosegow. His heart pulsed quicker every time he thought about it. *20,000 Years in Sing Sing. Castle on the Hudson. The Last Mile. San Quentin. The Big House. Each Dawn I Die.* What a tradition! Of course, those were civilian prisons which weren't quite the same as this. No. Harvey needed something a little more approximate to identify with. *The Great Escape? No*, that was a POW camp and Steve McQueen was far too blond. Edelman knew he could never solve the problem himself so he changed into his secret identity (one of six): Randall Crane of the Cinema. Well, Randall, what can Harvey identify with? That's easy, said Randall. *From Here to Eternity.*

Of course, thought Edelman. Why didn't I think of that before? I'm Frank Sinatra and Fowler is Ernest Borgnine. Wait a minute! I just remember why Frank Sinatra got the Oscar. He died.

'Lemme out of here!' screamed Edelman, rattling on the bars of his cell. 'I don't want to die. They're going to kill me in here.'

'Hey, Harvey, cool it.'

Edelman looked across the cell block where the voice had come from. It was Tommy Bennett.

'Hello, Tommy.'

'What do you say, man?'

'Tommy, they're going to kill me in here. Just like Frank Sinatra.'

'Hey, man, Frank Sinatra's not dead.'

'He's dead in the movie.'

'Oh, wow, Harvey. You're too much.'

Tommy Bennett vanished from sight.

'Are you all right?' asked Edelman.

'Groovy.' Bennett's voice floated up from inside the cell. 'I just collapsed against the wall.'

After the initial surprise of finding Tommy Bennett in the cell opposite his, Edelman stopped to assess the ramifications. Potentially he was imprisoned with the scoop of all time. Even Mr. Maxwell wouldn't be able to get this angle firsthand, I WAS TOMMY BENNETT'S CELLMATE' by Harvey Edelman. No. Maybe as a passing anecdote in some later volume of autobiography. He had no right to this story. Not *the* story. That belonged to Mr. Maxwell.

'Hey, Harvey? Got any weed? I'm starting to come down.'

'Sorry, Tommy, I don't— '

'*No problemo*. The little man'll be here soon.'

Edelman didn't know anything about Bin Vhan Ho at that precise moment but within half an hour he would know the whole story.

Maxwell turned up at the stockade later that afternoon and was ushered down to Harvey's cell. Edelman sprang up from his cot delighted to be reunited with his mentor.

'Are you all right, Harvey?'

'Yes, thank you, Mr. Maxwell. How did you get past Fowler?'

'Sergeant Fowler is no longer guarding the fortress. For some bizarre reason, he is now the communications officer.'

'You don't know what a relief that is,' said Edelman taking a deep breath. 'They still haven't found Captain Remington?'

'No. Probably never will.'

'And Ramirez?'

'Remarkably enough, I found Corporal Ramirez. He confirmed that Tommy—'

'Shh,' whispered Edelman. 'He's in there.'

Maxwell got up and walked over to the window in the cell door and stared across into Tommy's cell.

'Harvey, what's he smoking?'

'Oh . . . you know.'

'How did he obtain it, Harvey?'

'Bin Vhan Ho.'

'What is that without sub-titles?'

'A little old man. Works for Chy Ming.'

'Chy Ming is in on this?'

'As of yesterday. The old man came to visit and left a tiny pouch with a note inside from Chy Ming.'

'How did he get in here?' asked Maxwell.

'Bothered me for a while, too,' answered Edelman. 'But you explained it before. No more Fowler. Anyone can get by the rest of the Cowboys. Fowler's negative IQ is their total.'

Maxwell returned his attention to the heir to the HydroLux fortune. Why would Chy Ming want to get young Bennett high? Unless it wasn't Chy Ming but someone else using his name. No, that was out of the question. Even Claypoole wouldn't pull a stunt like that. He'd have no reason to. Under the influence of drugs, Tommy would only be more accessible. The truth would be found out. If Claypoole wanted the truth hidden sure as hell he wasn't going to freak out Tommy.

'Harvey, I want you to talk to him. Find out whatever you can. Tommy Bennett saw something in the jungle. Graham and I need to know what he saw.'

'What do you mean he saw something?' asked Edelman.

'Have you ever been stoned?' asked the correspondent.

'No, sir.'

'Well, you wouldn't understand but it's important. Find out *what* he was smoking on that patrol.'

'Is it going to be a hearing or a trial?' Edelman asked as the correspondent headed for the door.

'Fingers crossed for a trial,' said Maxwell as he waited for a guard to come get him. 'Mike Santiago is supposed to be arriving from Washington today or tomorrow to supervise this farce.'

'Is he the one they call the White House Watchdog?' asked Edelman.

'The very one, Harvey; administrations come and go but Miguel Santiago goes on forever.'


Fitzroy Claypoole was a shadow of his former shadow. Things were not working out at all. Oh, it was far from disaster time. Or as he had put it himself: 'The rubber rafts are out of reach but close at hand.' No, it was simply that the Colonel had lost control of the situation in the last twenty-four hours. This man Dundas had arrived and, despite evidence to the contrary, Claypoole was still convinced he was planning to take over the base. Then there had been poor deranged Private Edelman who had tried to paint a portrait of Father Doolan as some sex-driven hedonist. The good padre had pulled out his Beretta and had threatened to pump five biggies into the bespectacled Jew before the Colonel finally persuaded the god-man that Edelman's transgression was a military matter.

The Colonel had Edelman tossed into the stockade which left the base without a newspaper editor and six columnists. Cleet-boy had volunteered to take over the paper, but he was doing such a monumentally disastrous job as communications officer—he burnt all incoming telexes on principle—Claypoole had seriously thought of banishing the grizzly bear totally from his affections. The final straw had come only minutes before when an attaché phoned from Okinawa to say Mr. Santiago had forgotten his raincoat at the airport. Santiago was coming. Within two hours. Claypoole had never met the man known as the White House Watchdog but had spoken to him on the overseas telephone several times. He didn't like the man. He resented being bossed about by a civilian who wasn't his commander-in-chief. But Santiago spoke for that man. Claypoole was obliged to listen and obey.

The Colonel frantically attempted to get matters organized for Santiago's arrival. Special accommodations would have to be arranged. A car was needed at the airfield. Was a band appropriate? Was Santiago's visit official or unofficial? If official was 'Hail to the Chief' to be played out of respect for the President's authority? Or was one to play Santiago's favorite song? Was no one to be there? Someone had to be there, or the man would be stranded at the airfield. Curse Cleet-boy for burning the telex! The Colonel knew nothing about protocol for visiting celebrities. It had always been Remington's job. Curse Remington for vanishing! Claypoole was sorely tempted to sit down and make out his resignation papers. Retire undefeated and take the Cowboys with him. Cleet-boy would serve much better in a private organization. The Army was too big for him. Besides, Cleet-boy knew too much now, and heaven only knew what top secrets he was burning in the communications room. What grounds did Claypoole have for leaving the army before retirement? He was fit as a fiddle, strong as an ox, and a dozen other Popeye-like descriptions. If he'd only been less zealous about physical fitness. For the first time in his life, he wished he had asthma.

The door to the Colonel's office burst open and a tall, clean-shaven officer swaggered inside. Claypoole had never seen the man before, but he wore the uniform of a captain. The captain stood smiling insolently at Claypoole.

'How dare you come into my office unannounced?' demanded Claypoole. 'What about saluting?'

'I'm not afraid of you anymore,' said the captain.

'Goddamit!' roared Claypoole, 'I'm your superior officer.'

'I respect your superiority,' said the strange captain, sitting in a chair, 'but I'm not afraid of it.'

Claypoole sat and stared at this strange officer opposite him. Who was he? Why had he appeared now? Was this a trick of Santiago's to test Claypoole under stress? Maybe he was one of Dundas's men sent ahead to check the lay of the land. Possibly he was one of Chy Ming's men. Just the sort of thing that irascible bandit would try. None of these possibilities seemed right. After a few minutes there was something familiar about the strange officer. Familiar but different. The nose. The nose was far too small for a man of his height. And beneath his nose where a moustache had recently been—No! It couldn't be. Impossible. A man doesn't come back from the—

'Remington!'

'That's right, Colonel,' said Remington, lighting up a Camel.

'We thought you were dead, Burnie.'

'The *old* Remington is dead, Colonel.'

'Burnie-boy, you have no idea how glad I am to see you. The misery I've gone through these last two days. All this red tape. Dundas's arrival. Having to handle the press briefing. Santiago is arriving any minute. I don't know what music to play. There'll have to be another press briefing. I was about to hand in my resignation. Now you're back and everything's jake. I forgive you vanishing. Won't even ask where you've been or what you've done with your mustache. What I always say: "Every man is answerable to his own conscience." All I ask now, Burnie, is you get back to your job.'

'Don't want to be communications officer anymore.'

'That's your job, Captain,' said Claypoole, pulling rank.

'That was the old Remington's job.'

Something in this new, clean-shaven Remington's voice frightened the Colonel. Something that made him sit down quickly and nervously. This new Remington had no concept of fear.

'You—you've changed, Burnie.'

Remington laughed contemptuously: 'I've just been born.'

'What about Ayn Rand?'

'She's full of shit. The only thing I believe in now is Burnett C. Remington and the United States Army. I've had a good look at both these past forty-eight hours, Colonel, and I don't like what I see. Things are going to be different. Going to be a lot of changes made. Starting now.'

'Of course, Burnie,' said Claypoole, humoring his communications officer, 'We'll talk about them first thing in the morning. Right now you've got to get out to the airfield, meet Mr. Santiago and get a press briefing set—'

The Colonel was interrupted by the sight of Remington removing his revolver from his holster. He'd never seen Remington with a gun before.

'I told you, Colonel, I'm not going to be the communications officer anymore. I'm a soldier and it's time I did a soldier's job. We get all undesirables off this base. The first one to go is Maxwell. That seditious, socialistic foreigner. We get him out of here by midnight. And the rest of the press corps. They're interrupting our jobs. Give me a hundred men. Best we've got. Fowler and the Cowboys! I'll go up in those mountains, find Chy Ming and wipe him out and every one of his followers. Can't kow-tow to these peasants any longer. Get some of those bombs over from Okinawa. The big ones. Set off a couple just to let old Charlie know where we stand. And Hanoi. And Chairman Mao. We'll wipe the fuckers off the face of the earth.'

Claypoole began to tremble. His eyes grew larger in their sockets and his knees buckled under him. The Messiah had appeared before him. The day of judgement had come and honor of honors, holy of holies, it was an American Soldier who was to deliver them.

The Colonel crawled across the room on his knees and kissed Remington's West Point ring.

'Can you ever forgive me?' asked Claypoole. 'I didn't know who you were.'

'No time for any of that shit, Colonel. We've got a job to do. We've got to defend the world against the world.'

'Couldn't have said it better,' mumbled Claypoole, getting to his feet.

'We can't trust anyone anymore, Colonel. Revamp all our old ideas of trust. This base consists of you and me. Everyone else is under suspicion. We've got to have some kind of purge—'

'Yes, yes.'

'— find out who these people are. Get rid of them. Quickly and efficiently. This new concept came to me where everyone is responsible to the leader. Gives them something to work for. A mutual goal. A country is too vague an idea now. Can't put your finger on a country.'

'Know what you mean, Burnie boy. I know what you mean'.

'No, you and I, Colonel—'

'Call me Fitzroy.'

Remington grasped Claypoole's shoulders: 'Fitzroy, you and I will save the world together. Starting right here on the base this minute. The first one to go is—'

'Maxwell!' shouted Claypoole.

'Wrong! He's the second one. There's someone more important than Maxwell.'

'Graham? . . . Dundas? . . . Not Cleet-boy?'

Remington shook his head. He emptied out his gun, checked the chambers, then reloaded the bullets.

'First,' resumed Remington, 'we get rid of that filthy, perverted, degenerate charlatan. That so-called Father Doolan. . . . Did you know this "priest" has been having sex? With women!! I saw a naked woman in his cottage!!!'

Colonel Claypoole let out a moan: 'Oh, migod! What have I done?'

'What's the matter, Fitzroy?'

'Nothing, nothing at all.' answered Claypoole nervously. 'Nothing that can't be put straight.'

'It's Doolan, isn't it?'

'Ha-ha-ha. Innocent mistake. Burnie. There's been considerable confusion these last two days. But we'll get it cleared up. Just takes a phone call. Ha-ha-ha.'

The Colonel quickly recapped the incident of Edelman and Doolan and the fact that Edelman was now imprisoned for blasphemy.

'You see, Burnie. I just have to pick up the phone and—'

'Don't touch that phone, Claypoole!'

'Captain Remington, may I remind you I am still—'

'What?' demanded Remington, raising his revolver, and pointing it point blank at Claypoole. 'Hate to have to do this, Colonel.'


Who in their right mind leaves Mike Santiago stranded at an airport?

Santiago's office had sent a cable to the base announcing his arrival. Fowler had promptly taken the paper from the machine and burnt it. He was sure Pa would be proud of him.

When the plane touched down at the airfield, Miguel 'Mike' Santiago prayed that the base commander wasn't going to play 'Hail to the Chief'. Maybe a Burt Bacharach medley. Something cocktaily. Santiago wondered if there would be any broads available. He had meant to check who was on the USO tour that week. If it was that little blonde again whose mother used to star—Santiago was now at the front of the plane smiling politely at the idiot crew. The people he had to put up with in his job! He stepped out on the ramp. Where the hell was the band? Maybe they were in the lobby. But there was no one in the lobby. No one had come to meet Mike Santiago. Heads were going to roll.

Santiago nabbed a rather anemic-looking lieutenant from West Virginia and scared the hell out of him. The poor lieutenant ushered Santiago into an office where the White House Watchdog promptly devoured a telephone attempting to speak with Claypoole.

'What kind of Mickey Mouse base is this?' demanded Santiago, perspiration forming on the top of his bald head. He caught the lieutenant staring at his hairless head and Zapata mustache: 'What's the matter, son? Cat got your nuts? Grab a jeep or a Mustang or whatever you boy scouts drive.'

Major Dundas apologized profusely to Santiago and explained he'd also been trying in vain to contact Colonel Claypoole.

'Afraid the state of this base has been absolute chaos since I arrived,' explained Dundas. 'The communications officer vanished. Apparently one of a series.'

'Yeah, I know,' smiled Santiago. 'This guy Claypoole's a real laugh. Ever heard his slogans?' He held out a pack of cigarettes to Dundas.

'Thanks,' said Dundas, taking one. 'Why are you here, Mr. Santiago?'

'Make sure the court martial goes all right.'

'Graham got his trial after all?'

'Calvin Bennett got his trial,' corrected Santiago. 'But not a word till after my press briefing. Gather I may have to do it from a hot air balloon. Otherwise, no one will know I'm here.'

'May I suggest a drink at the press club?' asked Dundas, fully realizing the consequences of the two of them appearing there together.

'Major, you're no dummy. See why they picked you.'

Maxwell stormed into Graham's hotel room where the Murder Man was going over notes he had made that morning.

'It's like living on the bloody dark side of the moon,' the correspondent muttered to himself as he held Graham's jacket.

'What are you doing?' asked Graham.

'Santiago's here and he's holding a briefing in ten minutes.'

'What!?!'

Major Dundas had class. He didn't even attempt an excuse regarding the whereabouts of Colonel Claypoole. He conducted the briefing as though he were the base commander and promptly introduced Santiago 'who needed no introduction to the members of the working press'.

'You know him?' whispered Graham.

'Don't ask. I could tell you stories about me and Mike Santiago,' answered Maxwell. 'We used to work on the Trib together when I first came to America—'

'Shh.'

Santiago stood up on the platform and smiled out at the sardine-like press corps packed into the recreation hall.

'Hello, boys,' said Santiago with a weary intimacy as he stroked his Zapata mustache. 'Mr. Nice is here again.'

The press corps chuckled knowingly.

'You guys aren't going to like what I have to say,' continued Santiago. 'But it's from Pennsylvania Avenue and I've got nothing to do with it.'

'Bullshit,' murmured Maxwell.

Santiago read Maxwell's lips and smiled at his old pal. He continued speaking: 'The situation is quite simple, boys. Owing to the delicate and tragic nature of this case, certain special concessions will have to be made. Rumors have been floating about in the media that this matter would be dismissed in a simple hearing. As often happens in your instant and over-zealous business, you have failed to wait for official word. I bring you that word now.'

Maxwell shook his head in disbelief at Santiago's revival meeting style. It was too much. At least Maxwell could still be amused. Graham's impatience was reaching the point where the correspondent feared the Murder Man was going to throttle the information out of the Watchdog.

'Why the fuck doesn't he get to the point?' growled Graham.

'Let me get to the point,' smiled Santiago, 'and rid the room of unnecessary suspense. There will be a general court martial convening Monday morning—'

'Yahoo!'

Everyone stared at Frank Graham, who had fallen back on a traditional Wyoming triumphant hoot. The Murder Man slumped down in his chair and let the Watchdog continue.

'However,' continued Santiago, 'I'm going to have to disappoint you gentlemen with those "special concessions" I mentioned . . . In all due fairness and conscience and keeping in mind the extremely private and emotional nature of the testimony that will be delivered and on the advice of various respected and award-winning members of the medical profession—'

Maxwell sensed something was coming. Some god-awful twist of fate. Some dirty joke of destiny. Samoa wasn't that far away. That was where Robert Louis Stevenson almost recovered from his tuberculosis only to die of a ruptured blood vessel in the brain at age forty-four. Santiago, please don't!

'—we have decided the court martial will be conducted behind closed doors. There will be no TV cameras to inhibit the witnesses and the prisoner. The exclusion of television cameras also extends unfortunately to members of the press as well. The government does not wish this case prejudiced . . . There will, of course, be a complete transcript of the court

martial available at an appropriate time after the verdict has been reached
. . . That's all for this morning, gentlemen. My apologies once again but
I'm sure you can understand our position.'

The vanguard of disgruntled and disappointed newsmen trudged out of
the rec hall, across the parade ground, and over towards the press club.

Maxwell and Graham, however, leaped furiously up on to the platform
and cornered Santiago and Dundas.

'What kind of a sadistic prick are you, Santiago?' asked Maxwell.

Santiago turned to Dundas and said with a big smile: 'See why I love
this man? He treats me the same. My prestige has never gone to his head.
If he thinks I'm a prick, he calls me a prick. What's the matter, sweetheart?'

'You know bloody well what's the matter, you bald-headed son-of-a-
bitch! You just torpedoed me.'

'There'll be a transcript,' said Santiago.

'I don't want the bloody transcript. You can't lock me out now, Mike.
I broke this bloody story.'

'David, what do you want me to do? If I let you in, I must let everyone
else in.'

'Don't give me that rot, Mike. You owe me something. Who took your
ugly sister to her freshman prom in 1958? Who sat in fifteen doctors'
offices with you trying to keep your hair from falling out? Who helped you
move a body from the Bronx to the Taft Hotel so we could be closer to the
office?'

'Shh. Shh,' said Santiago. 'They still haven't solved the case.'

'The Tanzer Case?' asked Graham.

'No comment,' said Maxwell and Santiago as one. The two ex-Trib
staffers laughed at the memory.

'We had a lot of fun,' said Santiago.

'Then in the memory of the fun we had, give me a break. Because if
you don't, I am going to employ every devious tactic at my command to
humiliate the government and the authority of this trial. Who are you
joking with this postdated transcript? How do we know there'll be one
word of truth in what's finally released? The witnesses and poor Frank'll
probably vanish just like everyone else. Don't smile so patronizingly,
Major Dundas. They aren't going to leave you around unattended. No
one's going to be safe. Unless we share.'

'I don't know whether a lot of you rubbed off on me or a lot of me rubbed off on you,' said Santiago, 'but that's one of the greatest pitches I've heard in years.'

'"Words before blows,"' murmured Dundas.

'"Not that we love words better, as you do,"' said Graham picking up his cue.

'"Good words are better than bad strokes,"' said Dundas, returning the serve.

'Would you knock off the bloody Shakespeare for a minute?' asked Maxwell. 'We have a small problem here.'

'May I make a suggestion?' asked Major Dundas, in his best basso.

Six eyes fell on the prosecutor.

'It would be unwise to have the members of the press present,' said Dundas. 'But I'm sure there will be a considerable brouhaha concerning their complete lack of representation. Why not have one man represent them all?'

'How could such a man be chosen fairly?' asked Santiago, staring into Maxwell's eyes. The correspondent was convinced it was Santiago's long-awaited revenge for all the cracks about his bald head.

'Your main reaction will be from the American media. Pick someone who isn't an American,' continued Dundas. 'Someone whose integrity is beyond reproach. With no political affiliations whatsoever.'

'That lets you out, sweetheart,' said Santiago, pinching Maxwell's cheek. 'We all know who's paying your check.'

'I quit!' said Maxwell desperately. 'As of this minute. I'll send a cable to Frawley, Bennett, OmniPress, whomever you want. I'm a fair witness representing the world. Period.'

'You'd give up all that loot?' asked an unbelieving Santiago.

'Mike, I never wanted anything so badly in my life. Don't make me beg.'

'All right, you got it.'

'Just like that?'

'Why not?' asked Santiago with a serene smile. 'You, David Maxwell, will be the only representative of the press at the court martial of Thomas Jefferson Bennett.'

'What are you up to?' asked Maxwell.

'For God's sake, David,' interrupted Graham. 'He's giving you what you want.'

'Don't let the smile fool you, Frank. I know this man of old. He gave me my first silk hat. Keep smiling. Miguelito, but I'm keeping my watch on.'

The tail-end of Maxwell's sentence was interrupted by the rising and falling of a siren.

'That an air raid?' asked Santiago. They weren't supposed to have air raids during Santiago's visits.

'Not sure,' said Dundas heading towards the doors. He called out to Graham. 'Come on, Captain.'

'Do I have to fight?' asked the Murder Man.

The four men stared out at a scene of absolute chaos on the parade ground. The Montana Cowboys were driving their jeeps up in front of the admin building and jumping out armed with heavy mortar, bazookas, grenades, and generally enough weapons to besiege a city for two weeks. One overzealous Cowboy tossed a grenade through an open window. Cleet Fowler promptly kicked the man's teeth out. A few seconds later machine gun fire burst forth from inside the admin building.

'What's happening, Sergeant?' Dundas called out to Fowler.

'It's Pa!' cried Fowler. 'They got Pa!'

Within a few minutes, it became apparent to everyone that Burnett C. Remington had gone berserk, staged a one-man coup, and had taken over the base.

# THE BANDIT

Larsen stared at himself in the mirror: an ageing gun runner looking for an old-fashioned war.

His legs hurt and his fingers were numb. He needed a drink. Either that or a good fuck. But Cashbox was no longer available. Little Cashbox. Fantastic ass. Her cheeks fit into his palms so perfectly. And head! After thirty years in Spain, Africa, Latin America—every conceivable trouble spot—Larsen had never been fressed the way this kid did it.

Larsen pulled a dark turtleneck over his head and put on his fatigue jacket. He was tired. Too tired. After the Chy Ming business, maybe he'd call it quits. And do what? They just weren't fighting his kind of war anymore. It had taken him close to three years to get in on this action.

Larsen remembered the boat. And the priest. Just a kid. Staring at his tattoo. Then dropping dead. Heart attack. Larsen kneeled down and looked at his papers. The kid's name had been Doolan. On his way to Saigon to be a chaplain at the base.

Get yourself a new boy, Yang. The idea appealed to Larsen. He took the kid's collar and papers and rolled the remains of the real Father Doolan overboard.

Larsen ended up liking the priest racket. Straightening kids out without being accused of sticking his nose in. He established a system of universal confession— as long as no one squealed about it. It was a nice kind of life and he'd almost forgotten about Chy Ming, the legendary hero he'd come looking for only half believing he really existed.

But there *was* a Chy Ming. Larsen soon found himself divided between hearing confessions and teaching mountain peasants how to use the weapons he smuggled in to them by night.

Larsen checked the clip on his Beretta. Okay. Chy Ming wanted to see Maxwell that night. Larsen hoped he wouldn't have trouble with the Englishman. Checking the clip again, he climbed into his jeep.

At the same time, Maxwell was waiting in a jeep outside the stockade for Frank Graham, who was inside obtaining the release of Harvey Edelman.

A few seconds later Edelman walked out of the stockade waving his clenched hands over his head like a prize-winning boxer. Graham walked behind him beaming proudly.

'Sorry we couldn't get you a band.' said Maxwell.

'It's okay,' said Edelman, taking a deep breath. 'God, it's good to be out again! Fresh air, room to walk— '

'Don't milk the scene,' said Graham. 'You were only in for two days.'

Edelman hopped in the back of the jeep. Graham resumed his place in the driver's seat beside Maxwell.

'Shall we buy Harvey a drink?' asked the Murder Man.

'Why not?'

Maxwell directed Graham into town. As they rode along, Harvey was informed of the day's spectacular events.

'What happened to Captain Remington?'

'He got your cell,' replied Maxwell. 'Fitzroy wanted to kill him on the spot but Dundas insisted he stand trial.'

'Did you believe that Dundas?' asked Graham. 'The way he mobilized the Cowboys and recaptured the building. He's supposed to be a lawyer, not a soldier. Bet you he plays bridge, too. I hate guys that can do everything.'

'But what happened to Remington?' repeated Edelman. 'I mean *why*?'

'He flipped his lid,' said Graham.

'No,' said Maxwell. 'Not that easy. It seems old Burnie tried to steal a car the night we had the little encounter with him in the restaurant. After he made his fantastic exit, he got busted and tossed into jail for two days. The drunk tank. Except they aren't all drunks. Some very strange gents in there.'

'Who told you this?' asked Graham.

'Santiago. He and Dundas spent two hours trying to calm Claypoole down and get the story out of him.'

'But what happened to Remington?' Edelman persisted.

'Somebody did the old Indian rope trick,' said Maxwell. 'Except Remington smoked it. Joined the ranks of the stoned cold soldiers and had himself the ego trip of all time. Turned him into a super patriot.'

'I never heard of grass doing that,' said Graham.

'It wasn't grass,' explained Maxwell. 'It was some kind of roots and twigs mixed. Apparently, it's the closest natural, non-chemical hallucinogenic one can take before you get into chemically concocted mind benders like acid.'

'Malay bush,' said Edelman.

'What?'

'Malay bush,' repeated Harvey. 'Grows in Malaya. Unrefined. Twigs, seeds, everything.'

'When did you become a pharmacopoeia?' asked the correspondent.

'It's what Tommy was smoking.'

'Frank, stop the jeep!'

Graham pulled the jeep over to the side of the road. Maxwell was deep in concentration.

'You told me to find out,' said Edelman.

'Shh! Shh!' said Maxwell. A few seconds later a big grin crossed his face. 'Harvey, take a raincheck on that drink. Frank, let's get back to the base. I've got your defense.'


Things were relatively tranquil at Colonel Claypoole's house considering events of the afternoon. Santiago and Dundas sat in the living room sipping brandy as Dr. Renfrew came out of the bedroom.

'How's the patient, Doctor?' asked the Watchdog.

'He'll be fine in the morning,' answered Renfrew. 'Sergeant Fowler's going to stay with him this evening. Amazing how devoted he is to his commanding officer. Could have sworn he called him "Pa".'

'You know what they say about soldiers,' said Santiago.

'What do they say?' asked Dundas.

'Nothing personal meant, Major,' said the Watchdog. He turned to Renfrew. 'We'll see you later, doc.'

'Are you gentlemen leaving?' asked Renfrew.

'No.'

Renfrew took Santiago's hint and left.

'Major,' said Santiago, helping himself to more of Claypoole's brandy, 'this is a very up-tight base and will continue to be so until we get this business out of the way.'

'Considering your new plan,' replied Dundas, letting Santiago refill his glass, 'we can probably have everything settled by the end of next week. No loose ends. No scandal . . . But Maxwell isn't going to like your little surprise.'

'Leave Bonnie Prince Charlie to me. He's neither prosecuting nor defending. He has no say.'

Inside the Colonel's bedroom, Cleet Fowler maintained a steady vigil. Occasionally the Colonel would moan and Fowler would mop his brow.

'Cleet-boy.'

'Yes, Pa.''

'Promise you'll never leave my side after this. Day or night.'

'I promise, Pa.'

'Starting tomorrow I want a triple guard on Remington day and night.'

'He won't escape, Pa.'

'I'm not worried about escape. He's going to rot in there, Cleet-boy. He's never getting out. Ever.'

'Burnie's sorry, Pa. He told me. He's his old scaredy-cat self again.'

'He'll stay in there—'

'Till hell freezes over?' asked Cleet.

Claypoole beamed proudly at his grizzly bear: 'That's right, boy.'


Frank Graham walked along in the clean evening air. From somewhere in his memory came the phrase: 'I always walk. I never run. Jaunty, jolly.' Jaunty. Jolly. It was the jolliest and jauntiest the Murder Man had felt in months. He'd just left Maxwell and their conference had been inspired. Between them they'd come up with the defense of the century. Of course, it was Graham who would get all the credit. He was the one who would say it.

Graham could see the faces of the officers of the court as he melted their flint hearts with the harrowing and compelling story of Private Thomas Jefferson Bennett left alone by his comrades to standing his lone jungle vigil. With only his machine gun and a pack of Camels to keep him company. But this was no war film. There were no Camels. Just cigarette paper and—darn! He'd left the tobacco back at the base. The private's nerves were on edge. Out there—somewhere— lay the treacherous Viet

Cong. Perhaps his comrades had already fallen victims to their inhumanities. He needed a smoke. Then he noticed some jungle leaves. Better than nothing . . . How was this young soldier, the only son of a fine and respected family, a prize-winning track-and-field honor graduate from Yale, to know these were not ordinary leaves but those with a strange power to cloud men's minds? To create hallucinations. Make things seem what they were not. In fact, they led Private Bennett to believe his own comrades, 'his best friends on earth' were members of the deadly Viet Cong.

Private Bennett was a good soldier trained to kill the enemy. No longer in control of his reason, he responded automatically and without question to his training. He killed 'the enemy' . . . The tragedy, of course, was in who that 'enemy' really was.

Cut and print. All in one take. Wrap it up after lunch. Graham wasn't quite sure how he would word the final summation but that was no great problem. He and Maxwell would have the weekend for that. It really didn't matter what he would say. With the 'A' material and his voice, Tommy Bennett was as good as free.

Maxwell realized he wouldn't get the immediate reaction and plaudits. Graham would but the Englishman's triumph would last longer. When Frank Graham's voice was a memory, Maxwell's book about *the* story would be in its five hundredth printing. Squeezed on bookshelves between *Gone with the Wind* and *The Bible*.

Sex, thought Maxwell. Who needs it? There wasn't a woman on earth to compare with a beautifully constructed phrase. They would be his new loves: Maxine Metaphor, Sybilla Simile, Helena Homonym; they were his and he was loyal to each one.

Mapping out the chapters of the book in his mind, he did a thorough job up to chapter three. His thoughts galloped past the text and into the reviews. How could the critics not like it? It was all truth. Truth out of self-sacrifice (Maxwell submitted his resignation to *Insight*); truth out of loss (Cashbox); truth out of humility (begging Santiago and, to a lesser degree, collaborating with Graham); truth out of sharing (befriending and protecting Edelman). The book was more than a book. It had been a moral journey. As he reviewed —what? Notes. Ideas. But not one word written. Attaboy, Maxwell. That's really controlling one's ego. Bloody ingrate! Forgetting the basics: Artistic ego, yes. But total humility in approaching the text. No sense planning the seating arrangements at Sardi's when the show's still in Boston.

Where to start? And when? Should he wait until the court martial had ended and give a retrospective scope to the whole endeavor or do it as a daily journal? Maxwell sat down at his typewriter in a state of indecision. No sense sitting at the machine if he was going to go the hindsight route. Flip a coin for old times' sake. Fishing in his pocket, he discovered he had no change. He opened the top drawer of his desk and, amidst paperclips, pins, and staples, found a twenty-five cent piece and an old two-shilling bit. Maxwell was in procrastinator's paradise. He'd started off with the problem of flipping a coin to see if he would work or not. His new decision was what coin to use. Maxwell's games could sometimes be a definite pain-in-the-ass. This was one of those occasions. Choosing the right coin would carry with it a myriad of Freudian implications. Maxwell was about to give himself the new problem of selecting the method of selection when he shut his eyes and opted out for the children's favorite: Sky blue, sky blue. Who's it? Not you. Britain lost.

Flipping the quarter up in the air, he immediately decided on two-out-of-three if not three-out-of-five. If the coin landed the right way on the first shot, he might even go one-for-one.

The coin seemed to be twirling in slow motion (or perhaps it was Maxwell's mind). The correspondent never found out the outcome of the first flip because the lights went out plunging the apartment into total darkness.

'Bloody hell!'

Most of Saigon was asleep by this time and the neon had packed it in for the evening. Maxwell only had the three-quarter moon for illumination and he squinted furiously to make use of that. Getting up from his desk without difficulty, he managed to destroy his right shin on an unreasonably low coffee-table attempting to reach the house phone.

'Don't bother with the phone,' said a voice in the darkness.

'Aargh!' blurted Maxwell. He hadn't intended such an obvious comic book reaction, but he hadn't expected a power failure in the middle of the night accompanied by the mysterious voice.

A match was lit in a corner of the room. As Maxwell squinted his way towards the flickering flame, the match went out and the Englishman heard the voice say: 'Better put on a jacket. Kinda chilly up there.'

'Can't see a bloody thing,' mumbled Maxwell.

A new match was lit.

'Father Doolan!'

'Hello, pal.'

Maxwell stared at the smiling face of Larsen-Doolan holding a match in his left hand with the Beretta aimed accurately in his right.

'What do you want?' asked Maxwell.

'We're going for a ride.'

'What happened to the lights?'

'Knocked out the fuse box,' said Larsen.

'Isn't that a bit old-fashioned?'

'The old ways are the best.'

Larsen walked Maxwell down five flights of emergency stairs and into a smashed-up jeep parked by the service entrance.

'You and Remington ought to get together,' said Maxwell, staring at the military vehicle.

'It's Remington's jeep. He drove it into a laundry the other day. Perfect cover. Get in.'

Maxwell sat in silence as Larsen bombed the military vehicle out of the city and onto the mountain road. Unlike Remington, the god-man was in complete control of the machine—sometimes bordering on the impossible.

'Scared?' asked Larsen, after a rather remarkable hairpin turn.

'No,' said the correspondent, begrudgingly in awe of the priest's control of the machine. 'Where are we going?'

'Don't you know?'

'Look, Father Doolan or whatever your name is—'

'Larsen.'

'Are you CIA?'

'That's a hot one,' laughed Larsen.

'Where's Cashbox?' asked Maxwell.

'She no longer exists.'

'If you—

'Easy, hotshot,' said Larsen, fingering his Beretta. 'She no longer exists by her own choice. You really screwed her up, Maxwell. She thought she loved you.'

'Did she tell you that?'

'I was just a customer,' explained Larsen. 'She broke the house rules for you. But you and that goddam lawyer blew it. The two most up-tight characters I ever met. Christ! You make Remington and Edelman look like towers of strength.

'I'd rather not discuss it with you, thank you very much.'

'Getting frightfully English all of a sudden.'

'My heritage comes out whenever my basic human dignity is threatened. Second nature for you Americans to look ridiculous.

'The sun never sets, eh, pal?' snorted Larsen. 'I watched you guys lose the empire.'

'And I'm watching you lose yours,' retorted Maxwell.

'Don't know what you mean.'

'What are you doing out here, Larsen?'

'My health. I came for the waters.'

'What waters? We're in the middle of the jungle.'

'I was misinformed,' replied the gun runner.

'I've heard this conversation before,' said a bewildered Maxwell.

'Probably.'

'Are we almost there?' asked Maxwell, changing the subject as the jeep climbed higher into the mountains.

'In a hurry?'

'I'd like to know where I'm going.'

'Somebody wants to see you.'

'Look, Larsen—'

'Relax, pal. It's all part of the story.' The gun runner winked at Maxwell.

Two hours later the jeep came to a stop high in the mountains. Larsen jumped out first and tied a blindfold around Maxwell's eyes.

'The whole bit?' asked Maxwell.

'That's right, pal.'

Maxwell stumbled along a pathway for about ten minutes and found himself entering the mouth of what he took to be a cave. Larsen still hadn't removed the blindfold. Maxwell almost tripped at one point but Larsen caught him from behind. Finally, the gun runner removed the blindfold.

Maxwell found himself deep in the bowels of the earth. Great torches illuminated the cave all around him. Larsen called out in some Asian tongue and a young Vietnamese appeared with a pistol on his hip and a rifle slung over his shoulder. He spoke in heavily accented English:

'Mr. Maxwell? Chy Ming awaits you. This way.'

Larsen waved a finger to Maxwell.

'See you later, pal.'

Maxwell followed the young man down a winding passageway. The correspondent looked for bits of colored string to mark the way back, but the young guerilla seemed to know the route cold. There was no hope of escape. Talk about destiny. If one was going to die at least posterity had a right to know how. David Maxwell just couldn't vanish. Not in some labyrinth in South-East Asia. It wasn't fair. Even a plane crash was better than this. Of course, the trouble with plane crashes was never knowing who else might be on the flight. Three astronauts, two film stars, one secretary of state, and a member of the royal family—no way Maxwell would get any billing. He'd be an 'also killed'. Even that footnote would be better than this.

Following the young guerilla down a steep flight of ancient hand-carved steps, Maxwell was startled by the brilliant illumination that greeted him. The very walls of the cavern seemed ablaze. An underground river flowed through this part of the cave and the light of the torches bounced off the water and echoed off the walls.

The young man pointed towards the river then climbed back up the stairs leaving Maxwell alone.

Maxwell saw the bandit wearing a waistcoat of animal hides seated at a table beside the river staring at some maps and frequently jotting things down in a notebook.

'Be with you in a second,' the bandit called over his shoulder.

It was not an Asian voice. Probably another soldier-of-fortune like Larsen acting out some childhood fantasy. What was the deal with the pseudonyms? Why did Larsen have to be Father Doolan? Why did this man have to be Chy Ming?

Chy Ming folded his maps, closed his notebook, stroked his heavy, drooping moustache, poured himself a cup of rice wine and walked towards Maxwell.

There was a sense of assurance and professionalism in the bandit's walk and a smile on his face as he advanced towards Maxwell holding his hand out.

'Hello, David.'

Maxwell was startled by the bandit's familiarity. Was Chy Ming buddy-buddy with all his prisoners? Or was Maxwell even a prisoner? Possibly a hostage? The correspondent's intuition had rejected these possibilities. He was experiencing no tingle of fear. No presence of personal danger. Simply a sense of bewilderment.

Stepping closer, Maxwell stared into Chy Ming's eyes. The Englishman felt it necessary to draw back a step and take in the bandit's face. It reflected the charisma that made the man a natural leader. Maxwell had never seen the bandit before, but the eyes—where had he seen those eyes? For a moment he was reminded of visits to the National Portrait Gallery. All those familiar faces from centuries ago and only the eternal eyes as a link. But Chy Ming was alive and spoke with a familiarity and intimacy that could not be assumed.

'Have some rice wine,' said Chy Ming.

Maxwell followed the bandit to the edge of the illuminated river where a jug of wine rested on the table. The Bandit poured another cup and gestured for the correspondent to sit down.

The two men held their cups up in a silent toast and sipped the sweet, potent liquid. The lights of the underground river bounced off the bandit's face in an eerie and tantalizing manner. As though the blindfold had only then been removed from his eyes, Maxwell recognized the bandit. It was incredible. Impossible. Chy Ming was Milton Markson.

'Only now'?' asked Markson in his foghorn voice as he read Maxwell's thoughts.

'Yes,' gasped the correspondent. 'Is it really you, Milton?'

'The body was given to Milton Markson but meant for Chy Ming.''

'What happened?'

'Seems so long ago,' said Markson. 'Fowler and the Cowboys came to get me one night. They took me off into the jungle. Bound and blindfolded. Then they abandoned me. I was there for days, months, years. Maybe it was minutes. Then some people found me and took me to their village. It must have been a few days because I needed a shave. They brought me back to life and fed me. They shared their lives with me. Some of them spoke French so we could communicate—just. But we didn't need words. We'd sit by the fire at night and smoke. At first, I tried to explain to them about cancer. It seems quite funny looking back on it . . . Anyways that first time I seemed to get right outside myself and saw who I really was. Which wasn't anyone very inspiring. Then they told me the legend of Chy Ming. They began to think I was the stranger of the legend, and I came to believe it, too. I don't believe in magic, David, or any of that abracadabra crap. But I believe that I *was* meant to be Chy Ming.'

Maxwell sat as if in a trance. He couldn't believe this man had *ever* been Milton Markson. Not the Milton, who'd nursed his crabs, worn glasses, and lived in sexual fear of Estelle. Not this triumphant stoned cold soldier who was the military and spiritual hope for the people of Viet Nam. Maybe Maxwell had freaked out as well. But on what? No. Chy Ming Markson was simply a part of his moral journey. His personal, non-chemical, truth trip. Where did Maxwell fit in? Why had Markson sent for him?

'Afraid I've had you watched,' apologized Markson. 'Ever since I've been up here. You were my friend, David; probably the only friend I had in my up-tight former life. Should have listened to you. Then our roles became reversed. I found release while you became more engrossed and enmeshed in the Wichita Ball Club.'

'What are you trying to say, Milton?'

'Don't want to lay too much on you at once. Come. Let's eat. Want you to meet Yvette.'

The former doctor and patient walked along the edge of the underground river. While they walked Markson continued to rap about his new existence.

'Yvette is the most wonderful thing that ever happened to me,' said Markson. 'Through her I finally realized what love is. Been going on for millions of years. It waited for us to catch up with it. When I think how people abuse it. People like Estelle, who use it as a weapon. My wife is an evil woman, David. An evil, war-mongering emasculating woman.'

They reached a point farther down the river where a round, wooden table about a foot from the ground was covered with food. Various hides and animal furs surrounded the area. Markson removed his boots and gestured for Maxwell to dispose of his shoes.

'Have you made any attempt to contact Estelle?' asked Maxwell.

'Estelle can survive without me.'

'And your children?'

'They're not my children. They're hers. Ah! Here's Yvette.' Markson got to his feet.

Maxwell rose instinctively and had his second shock of the day.

'You didn't know my real name was Yvette,' said Cashbox. The girl put her arm around Markson and kissed him quickly. The three sat down.

'I told you I'd find Chy Ming, David. I'm sorry. He's what I've been looking for all my life. When Doolan finally made contact, I made him bring me up here.'

Maxwell said nothing but let the other two talk during the meal.

'Through Yvette I've learned the meaning of love,' said Markson. 'The true reason for having a child. Our values are all wrong and we have the Orientals to blame for it. The business of ancestor worship. Perpetuity of the line. There's no place in that for love. A child is the supreme token of love. When there are no more words of adoration to be said and all physical demonstrations of love have been exhausted, a child is the only natural expression. That's why it is so wrong for parents and people to stand in a child's way. To expect things from that child and to expect the child will allow them to dominate. When they do this, they forget the ideal behind the child's existence.'

'Estelle is the perfect example,' continued Markson. 'She wanted children for all the wrong reasons. She made us wait until my practice was established and the money was coming in. I wanted children sooner because I loved her. She couldn't understand that. Because she didn't love me. Not really love. Yvette and I will have children. All the children we can.'

Maxwell finally broke his silence: 'Milton, you can't go balling some chick day and night just because you love her. The world's overpopulated as it is.'

'They were doing it for the wrong reasons,' answered Markson.

'Perhaps. But we can't start from scratch.'

'We may have to,' said Markson.

'Milton, do you realize what you are? What you've become? The first guerilla hippy. I'm not being facetious. You can't go on fighting like this. Claypoole will give Fowler and the Cowboys full authority to come up here and blast you out of existence.'

'That's why I've decided to end the raids' said Markson. 'Why I've sent for you. Both of us.'

'Come live with us.' said Cashbox. 'Share our existence. Send for Audrey. You still love her.'

'We haven't found the end of this cave yet,' interjected Markson. 'It seems to go on forever like a Jules Verne story. They'll never find us here.'

'You don't understand,' said Maxwell.

'I do, David,' said Markson. 'I know all about Bennett and Graham and *the* story. Get out of it while you can. Before it destroys you. It's not worth it.'

'What are you talking about?'

'I *know* what Tommy Bennett saw in the jungle.'

'Tell me,' said Maxwell.

'You don't want to know, David. Believe me. I'm still trying to burn it from my memory. Stay here with us!'

'Milton —'

'Milton Markson doesn't exist anymore,' said Chy Ming.

'And neither does Cashbox,' said Yvette.

# THE TRIAL

It was Sunday afternoon when Maxwell returned to the base. Graham wept when he saw his collaborator.

'I was sure they got you' cried the Murder Man. 'And you were never coming back. What did they do to you? If they laid a hand on you—'

'I'm all right, Frank. There's nothing wrong with me.'

'Nothing?'

'Nothing.'

'You prick!' roared Graham. 'Where have you been? What's the idea of vanishing and not turning up till now? Didja find your little bimbo again?'

'I don't have to tell you where I'm going every minute of the day, Frank. Our relationship is getting slightly twisted.'

'Don't give me any of that chi-chi New York first-nighter crap. I know what you're hinting. Alluding I'm a little light on my feet—'

'Jesus Christ, Frank, I was only having you on!'

'Having me on what?'

'Sending you up. Taking the piss. Making a joke. Ha-ha.'

'It's not very funny, Maxwell.'

'We used to be on a first name relationship.'

'When we *had* a relationship,' retorted Graham. 'Before you went round the bend.'

'Now who's alluding what? I may not be the legal tyro you are but I certainly know grounds for slander.'

'Who called who a faggot?'

'Who's trying to have me labelled a nut-case?'

The lawyer and the correspondent stood and stared at each other. They had reached an impasse. It was impossible to walk away from each other after the words that had been exchanged. Something had to be done.

'Want to fight?' Graham asked finally.

'No.'

'Why not?'

'Don't particularly enjoy it,' said Maxwell. 'I get no pleasure out of knuckles grinding on skin making bruises and blood.'

'When you put it that way,' said Graham, 'I'm not crazy about it either.' The Murder Man took a deep breath and asked: 'Want to work on the case?'

'It is tomorrow morning, isn't it? Let's go back to my place.'

Maxwell made coffee and Graham sifted through his notes. While the correspondent filled the cups, he couldn't erase Chy Ming from his mind. The whole day prior to his return he had walked through the former Milton Markson's underground kingdom listening to his philosophy. It was nothing new. A blend of James M. Barrie, D. H. Lawrence, James Hilton with a touch of Ché Guevara—right down to the stethoscope.

Chy Ming was a true believer. So was Yvette. Enough to give up her fancy pad and hard-earned nest egg. Enough to go underground and have Chy Ming's 'real' children. Not the passionless brood living in America with Estelle.

What a glorious pipe dream! But that's all it was. How could Chy Ming have expected Maxwell to seriously accept his offer? With the crazy warning: 'We're sealing up the entrance to the cave soon. If you change your mind, you better get in touch fast.'

Maxwell remembered the drive back down the mountain with Larsen.

'He's planning to stop the raids,' said Maxwell.

'Yeah.'

'Where does that leave you?'

'Don't know,' replied Larsen. 'I was pretty happy for a while there. With the guns and the priest business. Don't know what I'm going to do.'

'What about Chy Ming?' asked Maxwell. 'And Yvette? Our little friend. If they seal up the entrance, they'll be dead in a month.'

'I know. They need loot. Regular. Once a month. I don't know where they're going to get it from. The Reds won't subsidize him. Neither will the Americans. I feel sorry for those kids. Wish to Christ I could do something for them. But I can't do anything for myself. I'm getting old, Maxwell. Old and obsolete. Don't understand the world anymore. No black and white. Just grey. Get so tired of everything, I'll stick this Beretta in my mouth one day and call it quits.'

Ten o'clock the following morning found Captain Frank Graham pressing his way through the throng of newsmen waiting outside the building designated for the court martial. Shutters clicked in tribute to his arrival and TV cameras whirred away.

Back in his element, Graham politely brushed aside the futile questions thrown out at him as he entered the building.

Stepping into the room where the court martial was to take place, Graham walked the set to get the feel of the place then popped back out to the foyer for a smoke.

Maxwell arrived a few minutes later and was greeted by good-hearted boos and hisses from the press corps.

The Montana Cowboys drove up on motorcycles in their official capacity as military police. One Cowboy slammed his brakes on too quickly and flew over his handlebars. The press corps cheered.

Fowler, who was guarding Claypoole in the limousine directly behind the motorcycles, broke the handle off the door in his attempt to chastise the fool cyclist.

'Scuse me, Pa,' said Fowler, crawling over Claypoole, 'Gotta get out and clean up that mess.'

'Don't leave me, Cleet-boy.'

'Pa, Arlo's got his brains splashed all over the sidewalk. You might trip. Won't be but a second.'

As Fowler got the other door open, Claypoole realized the car hadn't stopped. The Colonel gave the order to the driver, who slammed on his brakes.

The second car containing Dundas and Santiago promptly smashed into Claypoole's.

'That Claypoole is an idiot!' howled Santiago. 'He's going to get us all killed before the trial starts.'

'Patience, Mr. Santiago,' said a serene Dundas.

The TV boys, who had anticipated stock entrance footage at best, were having a field day filming the unexpected collision. Fowler was running around trying to smash the cameras while Claypoole wailed to get him out of the limousine.

'Are you with the bride's family or the groom's?' asked Edelman, who appeared at his heroes' side.

'How did you get here?' asked Maxwell.

'I got permission to stand in the foyer.'

'Do you know who's presiding?' asked Graham.

'Colonel Belknap from A Company. He hates Claypoole's guts.'

'That's encouraging.'

'Yes, only he's a little deaf.'

'That's all right,' said the Murder Man. 'If he can't hear my voice, at least he'll get the vibrations.'

Santiago appeared in the foyer a few seconds later cursing to himself and threatening to have Claypoole bounced from the service. He nodded curtly to Maxwell and Graham and headed into the courtroom.

A third car pulled up in front of the building. Tommy Bennett was led out escorted by two MPs. The guards paused in the foyer to allow Graham to accompany them. Maxwell followed a discreet distance behind.

'How are you feeling?' Graham asked Tommy once they were seated at the defense table.

'Okay,' said Tommy, nodding in a non-committal fashion.

Maxwell sat directly behind them and leaned forward to whisper a sincere good luck.

The officers of the court entered through a side door: four junior officers and Otis Belknap. Maxwell saw a distinct facial resemblance between Colonel Belknap and Ethel Kane Kirtsin. They had obviously been sired by the same eagle.

Court was called to order and Colonel Belknap proceeded to read the charge. Graham and Maxwell prepared to doodle through the preamble when they heard the craggy-voiced Colonel distinctly say Thomas Jefferson Bennett was charged with: '. . . illegal possession of drugs.' Full stop.

'WHAT!?!' roared Graham and Maxwell, rising as one.

'There will be order in the court,' said Belknap. He turned to the officer on his right. 'What did they say?'

'What,' answered the young officer.

Santiago leaned back against the wall in Buddha-like repose, admiring the rabbit he had just produced in the courtroom.

Maxwell dashed over to him: 'Duplicitous bastard!'

'Who is that man?' demanded Belknap, pointing at Maxwell. Graham had already rushed over to the correspondent.

'Don't fuck with the falcon unless you can fly,' crooned Santiago.

'David, sit down,' said Graham. 'You're only going to screw it up worse. We aren't finished yet, Mr. Santiago. Not by a long shot.'

When Graham returned to his seat, he noticed Dundas's eyes were down on the ground. The prosecutor had obviously not enjoyed this outrageous tactic of the Watchdog's. Okay, Dundas, if you want a real fight, I'll give you one.

'Colonel Belknap,' said Graham, rising to his feet, 'I respectfully request an adjournment until this afternoon so—'

'We haven't started yet,' crabbed Belknap. He looked out and saw Claypoole nodding agreement to Belknap's irritation. Fuck Claypoole, thought Belknap. 'You've got it, Captain.'

'What are we going to do?' asked Maxwell desperately.

'Keep calm,' said Graham, an old hand at eleventh-hour tactics. He turned to Tommy. 'Come on, son, we're going for a ride.'

Graham waved to the MPs and the guards escorted the Murder Man and his client outside to the limousine.

'What's he up to?' asked Santiago.

'Don't ask me, sweetheart,' said Maxwell bitterly.

'Come on,' said Santiago, good-naturedly. 'I've got a job to do. Besides, I was saving the kid's life.'

'And burying the issue,' retorted Maxwell.

'This administration is devoted to the policy of not rocking the boat. It doesn't need you coming along and being a shit-disturber just to win another Pulitzer.'

'Think that's why I'm doing it?'

Their discussion was interrupted by the arrival of Colonel Claypoole with Fowler not far behind.

'Couldn't leave well enough alone, Maxwell?' demanded the Colonel.

'Let me bust him one, Pa,' pleaded Fowler. 'I been itchin' to knock his teeth out since I met him.'

'May I remind you, Colonel Claypoole,' said Santiago, 'that I represent the President of the United States. You and your neanderthal thug had best lay off strong-arm tactics in my presence.'

'Stay out of this, baldy,' warned Fowler.

'Cleet-boy,' said Claypoole, growing a trifle nervous at his pet grizzly's lack of finesse, 'That's no way to talk to Mr. Santiago.'

'Bet your sweet ass it isn't,' smiled the Watchdog.

'I warned you once, baldy,' said Fowler, oblivious to Claypoole's words, 'now I'm gonna have to—'

Cleet Fowler had barely raised his fist when Santiago finished him off with three beautifully executed karate chops.

The Montana Cowboys' star pitcher lay on the floor gasping for breath with his 'Pa' sobbing fitfully over his grizzly bear's crumpled body.

Outside on the street, Santiago allowed his nerves to settle. Maxwell stared at his old colleague in awe.

'Where did you learn to—?'

'Suffice to say I know how,' answered Santiago. 'Just don't like having to use it.'

The Watchdog walked across the parade ground to the press club bar leaving Maxwell staring after him.

Inside the stockade, the MPs were escorting Graham and Tommy Bennett back to the latter's cell. After the guards had locked them in, the Murder Man made certain they were out of earshot.

'All right, Tommy. Where is it?'

'What are you talking about?'

'Bin Vhan Ho, Tommy. He's been bringing you Malay bush every day.'

'No, Mr. Graham. You're wrong—'

'Don't lie to me, Tommy.'

'I'm not, Mr. Graham. I admit I've been smoking in here. But not the bush. That's a bummer. Only had it that one—' He broke off abruptly.

'Where's the stuff you do have?'

'I'm out. The little man hasn't been here for two days. Been pushing like hell to trip but I'm coming down like a ton of bricks. I don't want to come down, Mr. Graham. I don't want to hear this shit.'

'Are you aware what Santiago's done?' asked Graham.

'Don't care, man. Just want to get this over with.'

'They've switched the entire—'

'I'm on trial for my life, Mr. Graham.'

'Hold it!' interrupted Graham. 'Trust me, Tommy, and listen carefully to everything I say.'

Graham left the boy's cell half an hour later convinced he had done the right thing.

Walking along the cellblock, he heard an urgent voice call out: 'Captain Graham! Please! Captain Graham!'

Ten pathetic fingers gripped the bars from inside the cell door. It was Remington.

'Captain Graham, you must help me. I'm the victim of circumstances. Outrageous lies defaming my character. That man Maxwell is behind everything!'

'Captain Remington, you attempted to take over the base. Don't you remember?'

'That's what Fowler said, Captain Graham. But I don't believe it. I'm a victim of some narcotics ring. Maxwell's behind it. He had those men give it to me in the jail. Please, Captain Graham, take my case. My family has money. They can pay. My name must be cleared. I'll die in here like Dreyfus.'

'Dreyfus was released. Emile Zola got him out.'

'Emile Zola's dead!' wailed Remington.

'So's Dreyfus,' replied Graham, attempting to get away from the deranged communications officer.

'Don't leave me, Captain Graham. You're my only hope. Maxwell will have me poisoned in here.'

'What makes you think Maxwell is trying to kill you?'

Remington stopped to think about the question. His mind hurtled backwards to the incident in the jeep. A huge grin of delight appeared on the communications officer's face. 'I know what civilian feet are!' he squealed with delight and began dancing around his cell. 'I know what civilian feet are!'

Before he could reveal the truth to Graham, the Murder Man had left the stockade on his way to pick up Maxwell.

Graham and Maxwell caught up with Santiago in a secluded corner of the press club where the Watchdog sat nursing his third Bloody Mary.

'You guys would have made a fantastic vaudeville team,' said Santiago, as the deadly duo sat down to join him. 'Say goodnight, David. Goodnight David.'

'Are you in any fit state to comprehend what I have to say, Mr. Santiago?' asked the Murder Man.

'Sit down, Victor Voice,' muttered Santiago. 'It's like listening to the "Best of the Shadow".' The Watchdog let loose with a ripe and fruity: 'In last week's episode, Margo found herself trapped in a room with the deadly Tong gang. Lamont Cranston was far away in an anonymous mid-Western city.'

'That's fantastic,' gasped Graham.

'I was a radio announcer for two years,' smiled Santiago.

'Really?'

'Frank, will you stop this crap and get to the point?' demanded Maxwell.

'Can't take him anywhere,' said Santiago. 'Regular life of the party.'

The Murder Man cleared his throat. He felt inhibited using his voice in front of an old radio veteran like Santiago. He played it simple and direct.

'Mr. Santiago—'

'Call me Mike.'

Dammit. Did the man have to be so pleasant?

'The situation is this, Mike,' said Graham. 'After a lengthy discussion with my client regarding the rather unexpected maneuver engineered by the court this morning . . . He's not going to let you get away with it. He demands to stand trial for murder. He will not be a part of the farce certain parties are trying to perpetrate. His strongest wish is to see justice done.'

There was a pause while the Watchdog dashed some Tabasco sauce into his drink. 'You guys are nuts. You know that, don't you?'

'Are you going to change the charge?' asked Graham.

'What do you want to make trouble for?' asked Santiago. 'David, I understand, but you're a puzzle. It isn't your kind of case, Frank. Believe me. Let me find you a triple rape in Kansas City. In an old folk's home. With arson tossed in. Possible homosexual overtones. At least fifteen dead. What more could you want?'

'A murder trial this afternoon,' said Graham.

'I blame you for this,' said the Watchdog, waving a finger at Maxwell.

'Don't start the guilt routine, please,' said Maxwell. 'We're dead serious, Mike. If we don't get that trial, I'm going on the air tonight and throwing the decision out to the American people.'

'Don't do it. David. POTUS will have you deported.'

'Don't try and bluff me, Mike.'

Santiago ordered another drink and stared at the two men waiting anxiously for his decision. The Watchdog waited anxiously for his drink. The thick red mixture arrived, and Santiago fondled the glass lovingly.

'What sort of work could the three of us get when this whole thing backfires?' asked the Watchdog.

'Does that mean you'll do it?' asked Graham.

'See you in court,' said Santiago glumly.

That afternoon a confused Colonel Belknap read out a totally different charge from the one he'd read in the morning. At first, Belknap thought it was all a scheme of Claypoole's to embarrass him in retaliation for calling an adjournment. When he learned Claypoole was in a state of total collapse in a hospital bed beside the badly busted-up Sergeant Fowler he realized the fancy footwork was that of the President's baldheaded troubleshooter.

'Let's get on with it,' muttered Belknap.

It was Major Dundas's turn to call an adjournment. He would need an extra day to revise his prosecution.

Colonel Belknap didn't really mind as it meant a full day he wouldn't have to bother with his hearing aid. The adjournment was granted.

Maxwell gave a briefing of the day to his press colleagues then took Edelman to a Saigon bar to buy him the drink he owed him. The private did not share Maxwell's high spirits.

'It wasn't right of Mr. Graham to con Tommy into that.'

'What are you talking about, Harvey?'

'Even if they find him guilty on the drug charge it would be a couple of years at most. Probably not that much. By pressing the murder charge, it could mean Tommy's life.'

'We're talking about Frank Graham, Harvey. He's never lost a case.'

'But we all know Tommy did it,' said Edelman.

'We don't know the circumstances. That's how Frank'll get him off. Tommy will get on the stand and tell the court how he thought the Ball Club was the Viet Cong.'

'How do you know that's what Tommy saw? It's only what you and Mr. Graham assume he saw.'

Maxwell was growing irritated with Edelman.

'Drink up, Harvey.'


Walter Dundas was brilliant. As the first two days of the trial progressed, Graham found his fear of the man change to admiration, then hero-worship, and, finally, love. How could Graham help but idolize a man who introduced maps? Crazy, complicated, pink, blue and yellow maps. Maps, whose relevance to the case were nil, but whose importance, when flowing forth from Major Dundas' lips seemed of greater consequence than the murder weapon. Then there were the ballistics. Dundas would bring in rifles, revolvers, machine guns and take them apart. He'd exhibit the pieces to the officers of the court and present them to 'his worthy colleague'. Graham loved the way Dundas called him his worthy colleague. As if he really meant it. Graham would gingerly accept the triggers, handles, and barrels held out to him as if they were the most succulent of Fanny Farmer's candies. In any other trial, Graham would have brushed aside these irrelevancies with the fullness of his voice. But he never said a word against Dundas.

Graham began to keep a scrapbook on Walter Dundas. He got hold of all the newspapers he could and cut out any quotes the Major had said. His favorite came from an interview Harvey Edelman had done in which the army prosecutor discussed the war.

'The war is a safety valve for our youth at home,' said Dundas. 'An outlet for their affluence. They have never known depressions, breadlines, or any form of hard times. They need this war. It teaches them healthy, democratic protest under society's benign and approving eye. It is a deterrent from the Fifties' boredom that led to hubcap stealing and "chicky races". If there wasn't a war for our youth to protest, we'd have to invent one for them.'

Graham never thought of the war like that before. To him, it was simply a drain on his tax dollar. He now saw it as a way of keeping children off the streets. No, that didn't sound right. It was a bad war. Dundas had to know that. Of course, he did. It was Harvey's fault. He'd obviously misquoted the flawless Major. Graham would speak to Edelman about it and make sure a retraction was published in the next issue.

On the second day of the trial, Graham placed Ramirez on the stand. The corporal repeated the same story he'd told Maxwell in Hawaii. If anything, it was a more moving account.

Dundas destroyed him in rebuttal.

The Major was a gentleman about the whole thing. One would never apply the word 'bigotry' considering Dundas's own ethnicity. But subtly—oh, so subtly—he confused Ramirez using big words, the immigrant soldier couldn't possibly comprehend. Ramirez said he didn't understand. He was unsure. Dundas hinted he was possibly unsure of what he had seen in the jungle. Ramirez grew scared. He started speaking in a jumbled fashion. Spanish words crept into his testimony. Then whole phrases. Dundas apologized to the corporal and said he didn't speak Spanish. Could the corporal please contain his statements to English. Ramirez began to tremble. Dundas touched his arm and told him there was nothing to worry about. This was an American trial, and, after all, Ramirez was a citizen. Wasn't he?

The last question was a master stroke. It hit the intended target dead on. Ramirez was terrified. If he said something this Major Dundas didn't like maybe they wouldn't let him become a citizen.

'I am not sure now,' said Ramirez.

'Would you like us to rule your testimony invalid?' Dundas asked politely.

Maxwell leaned forward and poked Graham in the back with a pencil.

'Frank, do something! He's murdering that kid.'

Graham stared at Dundas in awe. He knew Maxwell would never understand. How could he? He'd never gone through law school. Never stood up before a judge and jury. How could he possibly have respect and admiration for Dundas' art? Oh, Walter Dundas, you fool! Why are you wasting your time in the army? Come and join me. Be my partner. Graham began to doodle on his pad. GRAHAM & DUNDAS. He crossed that out and changed it to DUNDAS & GRAHAM. He didn't care about the billing if Dundas would work with him. Of course, he would never work with him if he didn't respect him. Graham knew the only way to win Dundas's respect was to beat him. By a knockout. No decision. The voice would not be enough. He'd have to have the goods and know that Dundas knew he had them.

It would have to be done quickly. The longer the case dragged on, the less chance he would have of impressing the major. Graham made his move the next afternoon. He wouldn't bother with any further defense witnesses. Just put Tommy on the stand and do his summation.

Graham made his intentions known to the court and called for an adjournment. Dundas nodded —impressed by the tactic—and left the building.

'Are you sure, Frank?' asked Maxwell. 'It's only the third day.'

'Come on, Tommy, said Graham, ignoring his collaborator. 'We've got to talk.'

The Murder Man sat in the cell while his client paced nervously. He'd been straight for the past thirty-six hours and was unhappy about it.

'Why did you let Dundas do that to Jaime?' asked Tommy.

'It's not a civilian trial. We don't stress objections and objections overruled. Everybody gets a chance to talk as long as they want. Which is what you're going to do tomorrow.'

'What am I going to say?' demanded Tommy.

'I liked you better when you were stoned.'

'You don't like me, do you?'

'I don't like your attitude,' said Graham.

'And I don't like the goddam circus this has turned into. Everybody acting for the cameras. Choosing their phrases so carefully because they know they're going to be quoted. We all know what I did. Let's get it over with.'

'We don't know what you did,' said Graham. 'We know you pulled the trigger. But why? What did you see out there, Tommy? When you smoked the bush?'

'I didn't see anything.'

'Private Bennett, I'm pulling rank on you.' said Captain Graham. 'It's an order. What did you see?'

'Seven members of my platoon and I shot them.'

'They were your best friends. Why did you shoot them?'

'I pulled the trigger and I shot them. I'm willing to accept my punishment. That's all I'm going to say.'

Graham buried his face in his hands. Then he tossed a cigarette to Tommy and lit one himself. He watched the proud, young man as he sat at the far end of his cot smoking unperturbed by the possible fate that awaited him the next day.

Goddam you, Thomas Jefferson Bennett, thought Graham. I'm trying to save your life. You're twenty-four years old. What do you want to die for? You're rich. Good-looking. Everything to live for. You can have anything you want. Just tell Belknap and the others what you saw. What monsters your buddies became. Leave the rest to me. We'll both be back in the States before you know it. I'll take you to Downey's and buy you the biggest steak you ever saw. There are girls back there, sports cars and skiing. I don't have to tell you about those things, boy. What do you want to give it all up for?

The accused continued to sit in silence.

The Murder Man knew he would have to get the testimony out of the Tommy without his assistance. He was too strong-willed. Graham couldn't break him under normal circumstances. He'd have to reproduce the same conditions that had existed in the jungle. He'd have to get Tommy high on the stand.

But first, he had to get his hands on some Malay bush.

# *THE VISION*

The next morning Maxwell received a call from the hospital saying that Colonel Claypoole was anxious to see him. Maxwell wasn't anxious to see Claypoole but there wasn't much else to do until the trial resumed at four that afternoon. Graham was playing the star and not accepting any phone calls in his room until noon. Maxwell hadn't seen him since the trial the previous day so knew nothing of the Murder Man's plans.

Crossing the parade ground, Maxwell noticed an unnaturally mournful Santiago. The Watchdog brightened a little and asked his old buddy where he was going.

'Got a call from Renfrew's office,' answered Maxwell. 'Claypoole's been asking for me all morning. Maybe you killed Fowler.'

'No way. Just shook him up a little . . . Come have a drink with me.'

'At this hour?'

'When did you sign the pledge?' growled the Watchdog.

The press club was remarkably quiet but then it *was* half past ten and the place had just opened.

'This is going to be my last case,' Santiago finally said.

'What are you talking about?' asked Maxwell.

'Funny feeling about it. We're all affected. You, me, Victor Voice with the pock marks. Getting bad vibes about this. Like we're tampering with something.'

'Sounds a bit mystical. You're just pissed off 'cause I shot down your wicked scheme.'

'No,' said the Watchdog. 'That was my job and kibbitzing with you. This is different. We're letting the genie out of the bottle, and we won't be able to get him in again.'

'You're serious, aren't you?' asked Maxwell.

'I haven't written anything in eight years. Nothing of my own. Maybe it's time I made people nervous recalling my time in the White House. No one would ever believe those stories, David. You can't imagine the absence of liaison in that place. Nobody trusts or confides in anybody. God forbid a member of the Pentagon should tell someone from CID what time it is. CID and the CIA can't stand each other. Won't swap information. Like little kids. The missile crisis? They both knew. If they'd shared the information sooner, we'd never have had to go up against the Russians. This asshole Claypoole is a prime example. Takes matters into his own hands and when he's in deep enough tells the Junkers in the Pentagon. They don't bother telling POTUS till it's a world-wide scandal. David, *we* found out when *you* found out.'

'What holds the place together?' asked a baffled Maxwell.

'Two empty Birdseye cans, several hundred yards of string and two million patriotic old ladies throwing darts at the map of Russia and listening to Bob Goulet screw up the national anthem.' The Watchdog stuck his hand in his inside pocket and pulled out a telex. 'This was delivered in the middle of the night. They want me to do a favor for the CIA.'

'Should you be showing me this?'

'Worst that can happen, we'll vanish,' laughed Santiago. 'Which is the subject of the telex. An agent was sent out here three years ago and never heard from him again. They want me to find him. Offer him more money. Unlimited expenses. Anything but defection. Nobody dies in Washington; they just grow old and defect.'

'What's your man's name?'

'Doolan. A priest yet.'

It was too good to be true. Just what Chy Ming needed. Unlimited cash. Larsen could write phony reports every month and, in exchange, get the loot for Ming and Yvette to live on with their underground community till the end of their days. A classic Hollywood ending. With the unlikeliest of people to play Kris Kringle: Mike Santiago.

'Think I know where this bloke is,' said Maxwell.

'Better tell me quick before I hand in my resignation.'

And before Chy Ming seals up the cave, thought Maxwell as he made his way to the hospital.

Maxwell was escorted to a private room where Claypoole sat in a wheelchair by the window staring longingly at the parade ground. He wore his familiar Noel Coward dressing gown with his cigarette holder sticking up defiantly in the breast pocket.

Claypoole wheeled his chair around to acknowledge the correspondent's presence in the room.

Maxwell was shocked by the Colonel's ravaged countenance. Within days the formerly peppy military leader had turned into a tired and frightened old man grasping vainly at his dreams of the past. The dramatic change must have been reflected in Maxwell's face for he heard the Colonel say: 'I don't want any of your pity, Maxwell.'

'Haven't said a word, Colonel.'

'I know that look in your face. Great moment for you, isn't it? Seeing an American soldier humbled and broken? How quickly you people forget. Who got you through the Battle of Britain?'

'Not you, mate. That's for damn sure. We sat that one out alone. Remember?'

'Go on. Gloat. One stinking triumph. Look what we did: John Paul Jones, Custer, the Rough Riders— '

'Detroit, Watts, Chicago.'

'We never fought there,' said Claypoole.

'Want to see the newsreels?'

'You don't understand us, Maxwell. Never have and never will. We're a peace-loving people.'

'And you've got to fight all the time to prove it.'

'It's people like you who push us into these corners with your fancy writing and arty movies and books.'

'I believe the phrase is "effete corps of impudent snobs". The vocal minority. The people who refuse to live in redundant box dwellings and lead the antiseptic, fantasy life of the Doris Day flicks.'

'Those are the *good* people,' insisted Claypoole. 'Don't make fun of them.'

'I've been making fun of them for years,' answered Maxwell, 'and lightning hasn't struck me down yet. Let me tell you something else, Fitzroy, Mr. Virtue Untarnished. If I had a choice between Potiphar's Wife and the winner of the Pillsbury Bakeoff, I'd take the Egyptian bird any day. Even if Golda Meir never bakes *latkes* for me again.'

'You're an evil, blasphemous man,' said Claypoole.

'Because I want to have a little fun and not be terrified your trigger-happy lot are going to push the button and open up one of those underground siloes, and we all end up burnt to a crisp defending your concept of freedom? What good does that do anyone except the little men from the next galaxy, who'll nibble on our ashen remains and decide we make a marvelous after-dinner treat?'

'I didn't call you here to have you expound on your nihilistic, hedonistic, live-live-live philosophy . . . I need your help.'

'You're a bundle of contradictions, aren't you, Fitzroy?'

'That is the second time within the last five minutes you've used my Christian name without my permission. Under normal circumstances I would have you disciplined.'

'The way you've buried Remington alive?'

'That is a military matter—'

'Or the way you handled Santiago?'

The Colonel began to gasp at the mention of the Watchdog's name. He wheeled himself towards his night table where he bolted down several pills followed by a flood of water.

'You're all in this together, aren't you?' demanded the Colonel. 'You, Santiago and Dundas. You're all trying to get this base away from me. Well, you won't. I'll be strong again soon.'

A glint in the Colonel's eyes betrayed the last sentence. He knew he'd never be the same again. He'd been having trouble breathing at night. The nose was going quickly. Only a matter of time before he'd be carrying Kleenex everywhere. Claypoole knew that Maxwell knew and grabbed the correspondent's arm in desperation.

'It's Cleet-boy. He's all I've got left. He and the Cowboys. We'll get out. Go to South America like you said. But he's got to be well again. You've got to help Cleet-boy get well again.'

'I thought there was nothing wrong with him. Santiago just knocked the wind out of -.'

'It's not that,' gasped Claypoole. 'He's got crabs!! My boy has crabs. He's in pain and none of the idiots here know what to do.'

'What can I do?' asked Maxwell helplessly.

'Help me find him.'

'Who?'

'Markson.'

Maxwell paused before he answered the Colonel: 'Dr. Markson doesn't exist.'

'That's not so,' said Claypoole.

'You told me so yourself, Colonel.'

'That was *then*. For tactical and security reasons, he could not exist. But I need him now. Please, Maxwell.'

'Look at me, Fitzroy. Look at my face. It's all backfired. Nothing's worked out. The man, Milton Markson, you speak of no longer exists.'

A flash of recognition swept across Claypoole's face as though he could see the underground cavern in Maxwell's eyes. The Colonel emitted a frightened whimper, broke away from the correspondent, and wheeled himself over to the window where he sat for the rest of the day mumbling epithets as a source of comfort.

Frank Graham's bathroom mirror reflected a very happy Frank Graham. Lather and all. A nice smooth shave for a nice smooth case. Have to look good for Walter. The Murder Man put on his freshly laundered military shirt and began knotting his tie. One would have thought he was going on a big date. Everything except the box of chocolates.

'Come in,' said Graham, as Maxwell knocked at the door.

'Couldn't reach you on the phone.'

Graham apologized to the correspondent for not accepting calls but needed his sleep for the big day. He explained his tactic to Maxwell when he was interrupted by a knock at the door.

A waiter wheeled in Graham's more than ample breakfast. The Murder Man asked Maxwell to join him and large quantities of toast and poached eggs were promptly devoured.

Harvey Edelman arrived a few minutes later.

'Have some juice quick,' said Graham. 'Need you to run an errand.'

'Before I forget,' said Edelman, handing the Murder Man a telegram, 'this arrived for you this morning.'

'Not another one,' said Graham, tucking the cable away in his shirt pocket. 'Either best wishes or more clues. Everyone's a detective.' He reached for another egg and asked: 'Where the hell is King of Prussia, Pennsylvania?'

'Why?' asked Maxwell.

'Got a telegram yesterday from some weirdo who said there was great religious significance in the fact that Tommy killed *seven* men.'

'Tightass Kelly is alive and well and living in King of Prussia, Pennsylvania.' Edelman was about to relate the misadventures of Francis Kelly when Graham interrupted him.

'No time, Harvey. You've got to find Bin Vhan Ho.'

'Why?'

'I need some Malay bush quick.'

'What for?' persisted Edelman.

'I'm an opium eater. Can't go into court without it. Just get the stuff, will you,' said the Murder Man growing impatient.

'You're going to turn Tommy on,' said Edelman.

'Smart boy,' said Graham.

'I'm not going to do it,' said Edelman.

'It's for his own good,' said Maxwell.

'No,' said Edelman. 'I don't think it is. You guys are doing this for yourselves now. You've lost track of the idea. Both of you. You're just after the glory now.'

Edelman was amazed at the words that came out of his mouth but not as amazed as Graham and Maxwell.

'When did you become the hero of this story?' asked the correspondent.

'Are you going to get this stuff for us or not?' asked Graham, getting to the point.

'No.'

'Come on, David. We've got one other possibility.'

As Graham and Maxwell started walking out, Edelman grabbed onto the Englishman's sleeve.

'Please, Mr. Maxwell. Don't do it.'

'Let go of my sleeve, Harvey.'

'Mr. Maxwell, it isn't right.'

'Harvey!'

'Please!'

'Fuck off,' said Maxwell, and hit the boy across the chest. Edelman's glasses fell from his face, and he kneeled to pick them up.

Maxwell stared down helplessly at the heartbroken boy. He wanted to say something but couldn't get past Edelman's wounded gaze.

'David, come on,' said Graham.

The stockade was in a relative state of informality since Fowler's hospitalization, so Graham and Maxwell were allowed to visit Remington without any difficulty. Maxwell even brought a copy of *The Fountainhead* as a peace offering.

Remington began screaming like a banshee when the correspondent entered his cell.

'Keep him away! Keep him away!' shrieked Remington. 'I thought you were my friend.'

'I am your friend, Burnett,' said Graham. 'So is David. See. He brought you a book.'

'He's right round the twist,' whispered Maxwell.

'Be nice to him,' hissed Graham.

'Burnie,' said Maxwell, holding the book out like a peppermint stick, 'who found the bodies for you? Remember? We were friends then. You said if I ever wanted a favor. If there was anything you could do for me.'

Maxwell had his arm around the communications officer and Remington was resting his head on the correspondent's shoulder clutching the Ayn Rand tome in his hands.

'You're never going to scare me again?' asked Remington.

'Never,' said Maxwell.

'Can we go trick or treating at Hallowe'en?'

'Whatever you want, Burnie.'

'I'll be Woody Woodpecker and you'll be Wally Walrus?'

'Of course, Burnie,' said Maxwell. 'But first tell us where you got the Malay bush.'

'I don't remember.'

'Please, Burnie.'

'No.'

'GODAMMIT, REMINGTON!!' shouted Maxwell.

That did it. The dam burst. Remington started to scream, shout, wail, stamp his feet, shit in his trousers, rock, faint— all at once!

'He lied to me! He lied to me!' wailed Remington. 'He's not my friend.' He started crying again.

'Get the hell out of here,' said Graham.

Maxwell stood outside the cell block while Graham soothed the tortured communications officer. Five minutes later Graham reappeared with the necessary information.

As the two men walked down the length of the cell block, Remington waved a long, skinny arm out of the door of his cell and chanted after Maxwell: 'Civilian feet! Civilian feet!'

It was two o'clock by the time Graham and Maxwell returned from Saigon with the Malay bush. The Murder Man wanted to check the lighting in the courtroom before he took the bush over to Tommy.

'Why the lighting?' asked Maxwell. 'There won't be any cameras in there.'

'The natural lighting,' said Graham impatiently. 'Through the windows. Got to see where it's going to hit my face and whether it's going to hit Belknap. Blind *and* deaf I don't need.'

The press corps were milling around the building unusually early. Although Maxwell had said nothing out of the ordinary to them in his briefing the evening before, the newsmen seemed to sense something big was going to break that afternoon.

Graham went into the courtroom and Maxwell stopped to chat with Santiago in the foyer.

'Don't bother talking to that guy,' said Santiago.

'Who do you mean?' asked Maxwell.

'What's-his-name. The priest. They found him this morning. Stiff.'

'Father Doolan's dead?'

'Couple of soldiers found him in his cottage. He'd blown his brains out with a Beretta . . . Saves me a lot of trouble.'

Maxwell felt as if a prize stallion had kicked him in the guts. He wanted to vomit but didn't have the strength.

He paused to think. About a lot of things. Coming at him at once. Audrey ringing him in the middle of the night. Still loving him. The film star having crabs. Milton not being able to ball Estelle. Chy Ming making love forever with Yvette. Santiago's presentiment. The genie in the bottle. Larsen putting on his trench coat, hiking up his trousers, tugging at his ear lobe. Here's looking at you, kid. Sticking the barrel of the Beretta in his mouth. What was the matter with the world, Doolan-Larsen? How had it changed? You could have had the money. We could have had a happy ending. What was the final sorrow for you? Was it a woman? Or were you just the last of the Mohicans? Your suicide is turning into a pact. I can't get through to them now. Chy Ming and Yvette will never know they might have been happy. They'll die up there. I didn't lie to Claypoole. Milton Markson *doesn't* exist anymore.

He thought of the trial. Tommy Bennett's testimony. The vision. Chy Ming's words came back to him. *I know what Tommy Bennett saw in the jungle. You don't want to know, David. Believe me. I'm still trying to burn it from my memory.* Chy Ming and Tommy Bennett had obviously seen the genie in Santiago's bottle. The thing the Watchdog feared would be let loose on the world. Maxwell realized this was the same evil genie that had whispered in Larsen's ear as his hand reached out for the Beretta.

Tommy Bennett must not take the stand, decided Maxwell. Not under the influence of Malay bush. He didn't know why but he had to stop Graham. Harvey, forgive me. You were right, you sorrowful Talmudic logician. We don't know the answer because we're not supposed to.

Maxwell dashed into the courtroom and found it deserted.

On the defense table lay the crumpled-up telegram that had been in Graham's pocket. Maxwell unfolded it.

ROCHELLE WAS MARRIED YESTERDAY.
BOCHNER

It was too late.

The officers of the court had entered the room. Dundas sat poised at his desk. Santiago sat in a corner of the room staring idly at the ceiling. He wouldn't look at Maxwell nor would Maxwell look at him. Maxwell didn't know where to look then discovered the same piece of nondescript ceiling. It was very peaceful around that area of greying plaster.

'Where are the prisoner and Captain Graham?' Belknap asked the court clerk.

Maxwell knew Graham was stalling. Waiting until the exact second before the drug would take effect. There would be no chance to whisper a warning to the Murder Man. 'Our souls like to a ship in a black storm . . .' Noise in the foyer. The smart clicking of the MPs boots. Graham marching in with Tommy. Not a glance sideways. Oblivious to Dundas, Maxwell, and Santiago. 'I have a journey, sir, shortly to go. My master calls me I must not say no.'

The boy was on the stand and Graham was being gentle and coaxing with him.

Thomas Jefferson Bennett began to speak:

'We didn't draw lots or anything. Grocowicz simply said, "Bennett, you stay here and guard the supplies. If we're not back in an hour . . ." He just let it trail off like that. Didn't really bother me because I figured they'd be back in an hour. We're not particularly noted for taking chances. Why should we? Patrols are like seeing how long you can hold your breath underwater. You do it if you can then come up for air. What does popping your lungs prove? Tell that to Fowler. Hey! How did I get on to Fowler?

Excuse me. I must have—Hey, Mr. Graham? What did you give me to? Ooops. Better keep stumm about that. Ha-ha-ha-ha. Don't think they'd approve. Anyhow, an hour went by. Or it seemed like an hour. I forgot my watch at the base. Got scared. I'm not ashamed to admit it. Anyone who says they aren't scared sitting out in the middle of the jungle with the Cong all around them is full of crap. Then I remembered the Malay bush we'd had the night before. We didn't have a chance to smoke it what with packing and all. None of us had ever had it before. Supposed to be really groovy stuff. So, I rolled a joint figuring it would calm my nerves down. Didn't want to wet myself or anything. Afraid to drop my gun long enough to take a pee. I just sat there on top of all the supplies and had a little smoke. It was a nice high at first. Like very smooth grass. Then it was like Disneyland, man. You know. Talking mushrooms and rabbits named Harvey. Wow! It was too much. You don't mind my rapping on like this, do you? You can shut me up when you want but it was just so nice. I can remember it now just like I was there again. Heyyy! What was that stuff, Mr. Graham? Ha-ha-ha. Oh, wow! Do you treat all your clients like this? The Murder Man got me stoned. Ha! Sorry. Got to tell the story. So I'm sitting there and I saw him, man, I really saw him. Sooo weird! After all those years I mean. Figured he must be sawdust by now. Or living on some reservation in Arizona with Princess Summer-Fall-Winter-Spring and Chief Thunderthud. But there he was. A little older but the same cowboy shirt, scarf, and boots. And the freckles. I said "Hey, Man, what are you doing here?" And we both laughed. Started rapping about old times. About the Flubadub and Dilly Dally and Mr. Bluster. And Clarabelle and the seltzer bottles. Duckburg, too. He knew all about Duckburg. I asked him about the Beagle Boys. Always worried about the Beagle Boys 'cause when I was a kid I was told my father was wealthy. I didn't know what that meant. 'Cause I was only four or five. Somebody else told me Scrooge McDuck was wealthy. So I could dig that all right. Then I got worried the Beagle Boys might rob my father. But they never did. They were too busy robbing Scrooge McDuck. He said Daisy Duck was still gorgeous and Gladstone Gander was still pursuing her and Gyro Gearloose was still living in sin with that lightbulb. He had this big bag—my old friend with the freckles—and out of the bag, he pulled Three Musketeers, Snickers, 5th Avenue candy bars, Necco wafers, Paul Parrot shoes, and Froggy the Gremlin. Too much! Plunk your magic twanger, Froggy! BOINNNG! Froggy was the same as ever. Apparently, he'd been living with Beulah the

Witch for the last few years. Which was cool 'cause I always thought he was all talk and no action. Maybe even gay. Like a certain Kuklapolitan whose name I don't want to mention. The three of us sat there for hours and it was great. Then Froggy hopped into the jungle and my freckle-faced friend asked me what I wanted to do. I remembered a rock concert not too far away. So we went there and on the way, my friend asked me if I still had a piggy bank. And I blew my mind. A piggy bank! Hadn't seen one of those for years. A big, fat, pink piggy bank that you loved like a brother but didn't hesitate to smash to pieces once he was bulging with pennies. But I hadn't had a piggy bank in years, so my friend said he'd treat me. Which was really nice. It was a very heavy concert. Really out of sight. Really good vibes. Everyone was swaying back and forth. But my friend didn't get it. He ran up on the stage and I had to chase after him. He stood in front of the kids and hit them with his old standard: HEY, KIDS!! WHAT TIME IS IT?? But they didn't answer him. I grabbed him and said "Sit down, man. They don't know you. That's Fifties stuff. That's I Like Ike and My Fair Lady. We're into the Seventies. They don't remember Howdy Doody." Howdy just stared at me. Could all those millions of kids have forgotten Doodyville? And he got old. Right in front of me. Really old. And suddenly the kids shut up. They saw Howdy was going to speak again. But it was a different voice. Like some old Shakespearean actor. And he spoke:

> *"But the king hath a heavy reckoning to make*
> *If his cause be not good: when all those souls*
> *Whose bodies shall be slaughtered here*
> *Shall join together at the latter day*
> *And say I died at such a place—"*

BANG! Everybody screamed and gasped as Howdy Doody's body crumbled to the floor of the platform. I rushed to him. He told me it was too late, and I should run for it. I asked him who did it and with his dying words he gasped "The philgrims". I ran like the wind. Just kept running. Someone was after me. I didn't know who they were. But they'd killed Howdy Doody and they wouldn't think twice about me . . . So I ran and ran till I came to a baseball stadium. I didn't recognize it but it was a stadium. Figured I'd watch a game and try and figure out what to do. As I went into the stadium something flew over my head. I looked up and it was a guy on a broomstick. With silver sunglasses. Dressed like the guy on the Quaker Oats box. Figured it was some kind of nut and went in to watch the game. The Cowboys were playing. They were in the field. Claypoole was standing in the dugout smiling. All those guys in silver sunglasses were standing behind him in long black coats and wide black hats. They just stood there watching the other team carried off the field. Then I heard two guys behind me talking about a rocket they'd just sent to the moon. They were whispering. One of them said: "They're all looking up. They'll never see the mess lying at their feet'' . . . I turned around and these guys had the same silver sunglasses and black outfits. I knew who they were. "The philgrims! You're philgrims!" They started chasing me. I ran out of the stadium and heard the noise overhead. They were following me on their broomsticks. Zipping down at me like dive-bombers. I found myself running through the streets. Past protesters and looters. I saw the President being sworn in. Then being shot. Then his brother. And everyone mourning. But not caring who really did it. And the war. Everyone arguing about the war. I wanted to stop and tell them. Forget about the war. We've got to stop saving other people and worry about ourselves. The threat is inside ourselves. People trying to get together and being frustrated. All this rushing about and frenetic activity. It's what the philgrims want. It's camouflage so you won't see what's really going on. And I remembered Gatsby. The desire for the whole world to be in uniform and standing at moral attention forever. Attention! Attention, please. But no one's listening. I ran past the warehouses with all the chemical poisons and jumped over the siloes with their underground rockets on full red alert. I looked down one of those siloes and saw the philgrims rushing about getting things ready. I yelled down for them to stop but they simply sprang for their telephones. Within seconds the skies were filled with their men on broomsticks hunting for me. I started running again. But I wasn't alone now. There was this hippy. I think he was a hippy. He had hair down to his shoulders. Moustache and beard. But a very gentle face. We ran together. Like training at Yale . . . We ended up back in the jungle. I couldn't breathe but he wasn't even gasping. We sat down on the supplies. My joint was still going. After all that time. I stared at this guy. He wasn't a hippy. He was Jesus. I know it sounds crazy. But it *was* Jesus. I asked him what the hell he'd got us into. How he could tolerate the philgrims. Their existence that was so opposite to the original ideals of the republic. He just smiled at me, man, and told me we'd screwed things up long before the republic. He didn't want to be worshipped. That was idolatry. And His Father didn't want to be worshipped. He wanted his existence *celebrated*. Life and existence should be a celebration, he said. He was appalled by the return of the golden calf and the moral cancer that was crippling the world. I told him to send some kind of sign. He just smiled and didn't say anything. He didn't have to. The signs were everywhere. But nobody wanted to know. I thought about that bandit, Chy Ming, who'd been smuggling the grass in to me. Where did he fit in? Why had he stopped sending me stuff? The philgrims must have gotten to him. They were omnipotent. But the frustrating part was I was sure we could be rid of them simply by saying: 'I will have no more of you. Be gone. Vanish.' But that was too easy. How could one disassemble a machine like that? They were too clever. They knew Man too well and could offer him too many pleasures and enticements. It was futile. The philgrims would chase Man into the grave. But not a quick death. A slow-malingering one. And in that last moment, they would spit in Man's face and say it was all a hoax, a sham, a waste . . Then I saw the boys coming back. Punjab and the Asp, prime targets for the philgrims. And Kip, poor Kip, so far from Sheila pledging his love in a latrine. And Fingers—so out of date still believing the golden myths of the philgrims. And Keller, and Big Ralph, and Buzz. Trapped in the mainstream. Dancing happily on the philgrim treadmill. I wanted to help them. But how? Tell me how to help you. And as they drew closer, I looked at their faces. They had the same expression on their faces Howdy did when he got his. The philgrims had been chasing them and were probably not too far behind. There they stood in front of me. My best friends. Holding out their hands and asking me to deliver them. Save them from the philgrims. I looked at Jesus but he had turned away. He knew what I was thinking. He couldn't condone it but He wouldn't stop me. In our own way, we would defeat the philgrims. We would be a symbol. A sign. But what the hell good is a sign in the jungle where no one can see it? People must come to attention. Whether they want to or not. The boys were waiting. I lifted up my gun and let my finger find the trigger. I heard no noise when it happened. They went to the ground in gentle slow motion. It was over. I looked up at Jesus. He smiled sadly at me then started to walk off into the jungle. A bullet ripped into my hand, but I didn't feel it. I kept watching Jesus walk into the jungle. Then I heard the philgrims overhead. Like buzzards come to a feast. And I felt cheated. As if the whole world was covered in a rug that had been pulled out from under me. I saw Jesus just before he disappeared, and I shouted after him: "WHY ME? WHY NOW?"'

A silence fell over the courtroom.

The Murder Man was far off in Wyoming watching stallions gallop against the free open skies. He saw a boy whom he recognized as the young Frank Graham feeding sugar lumps to the colts. A nice little boy with a high squeaky voice. Clear complexion. Scarlet fever had not left its marks on him yet. Get on the pony's back. Don't need a saddle. Ride off past the reservation. Past the general store and the newspapers from Cheyenne. Where was Madrid? Where was Munich? What was the Third Reich? Going to be a cowboy when I grow up. Someone's talking to me. That old man with the hearing aid. Wants to know if I'm finished. Oh, yes. Yes.

Graham mumbled some obligatory remark about the prosecution.

Dundas looked up as if the guilty finger had suddenly fallen on him— a verbal round of hot potato.

'The prosecution has nothing to add.' said Dundas. who had his papers arranged neatly in front of himself and waited like a claustrophobe for the doors to be thrown open.

Maxwell heard Santiago breathing heavily beside him. He watched the four young officers follow Belknap into the room where they would attempt to deliberate and come up with some sort of decision.

'They'll be out for a while,' Santiago said in a hoarse whisper.

A quiet had settled on the courtroom. There really wasn't anything to say. What *can* you say about a twenty-four-year-old boy who has just shattered the American dream?

Twilight had descended upon the base as Maxwell stood alone near the airstrip watching the Huey Cobra gunships coming back from their missions. The war had gone on as usual that day oblivious to the trial of Thomas Jefferson Bennett. The local Vietnamese were hurrying towards the choppers with sacks of black-market walnut shells to clean the clogging red laterite dust off the compressor blades. Maxwell had to laugh. Twentieth-century warfare. A half million dollars' worth of sophisticated machinery and the only thing that could keep it functioning was walnut shells. The philgrims knew their business.

Maxwell felt tired. He'd said goodbye to Graham and Santiago a few hours before. More like a few years. Everything seemed so far behind him now. He desperately wanted to sleep.

Wrenching his clothes from his body, he maneuvered his way between the sheets. Sleep—a long, deep, childlike sleep—came over him. There were no dreams. Nothing. Must be like this to die, thought Maxwell. I'm dying. *This* has been my destiny. To die in my sleep. Thanks a lot, philgrims.

The boredom of being dead was interrupted an hour later by an overseas telephone call. It was Audrey calling to find out what had happened.

'We lost,' said Maxwell.

'They found him guilty?'

'I don't know. Really isn't important. We lost anyhow.'

'I don't understand, David.'

'Oh, Christ, Aud, it's all been such shit. *The* story and *the* case and all this useless, purposeless hustling. For what? I can't remember the last time I was ever truly happy. Isn't that incredible? The ironic thing is that I had a chance offered to me to . . .'

'David?'

'Maybe. Just maybe . . .'

'Are you all right?'

Maxwell sat up on his deathbed and lit a cigarette. Fuck you, philgrims!

'Audrey?'

'Yes, darling?'

'Does the name Chy Ming mean anything to you?'

# ABOUT THE AUTHOR

Charles Dennis is the author of fourteen novels including *Balm of Angels, Hollywood Raj, The Magiker, The Dealmakers, The Next to Last Train Ride* and *Stoned Cold Soldier*. His plays *Going On, King Solomon's Treasure,* and *Significant Others* have been produced in New York, Los Angeles, London and Edinburgh.

For his company, Foo Dog Films, he wrote and directed the movies *Deadly Draw, Barking Mad, Chicanery* and *Hard Four*. His repertory company of actors includes Bryan Cranston, Patty McCormack, Brent Huff, the late Ed Asner, Ed Begley Jr., Neil Dickson, Kate Vernon, Fred Melamed, Ross Benjamin, Colin Fox, Michele Scarabelli, Mark Rydell, Ulrika Vingsbo, Pete Sepenuk, Nicole Ansari, Lou Wagner, Lianne Hu, and the late Ken Welsh.

Dennis won the Best Actor award for his performance as Franz Altman in the screen version of *King Solomon's Treasure* at the Studio City Film Festival. As a voice artist, he can be heard on such classic video games as *Doom 3, Star Wars, Star Trek, Call of Duty,* and *Skyrim*.

A respected film historian, Dennis has contributed to the *Los Angeles Times* and the *Hollywood Reporter*. He has done on-camera interviews and commentaries for the Criterion Collection. He is the author of *There's a Body in the Window Seat: The History of Arsenic and Old Lace*.

He is presently working on *People in Aspic* (the sequel to *Hollywood Raj*) and recording his books for Audible.

Dennis lives with his wife, producer/publisher/actress Ulrika Vingsbo, on their ranch in Shadow Hills, California with their three horses, a bearded dragon, a turtle and two Boston terriers named Sam and Steve.

Dennis can be reached at charlesdennisauthor.com.